The House of Frankenstein!

A comedy-horror

Martin Downing

Samuel French – London
New York – Sydney – Toronto – Hollywood

Please see page iv for further copyright information

THE HOUSE OF FRANKENSTEIN

Originally presented in London in March 1989 with the following cast of characters:

Baron Von Frankenstein	Michael Downing
Ygor	Ian Taylor
The Monster	Daniel Lambert
Frau Lurker	Martin Downing
Baroness Von Frankenstein	Tania Galloway
Harry Talbot	Neil Hitchcock
Countess Ilona Bathory	Janice Greenwood
The Phantom of the Opera	Peter Tarrant
Count Vlad Dracula	Mike Balmer
Isabel Channing	Victoria Potter

The play was directed by **Martin Downing**

The action of the play takes place in Castle Frankenstein, somewhere in the Carpathian Mountains

ACT I	Scene 1	Shortly before seven o'clock
	Scene 2	Ten minutes later
	Scene 3	A minute later

ACT II	Scene 1	Shortly before midnight
	Scene 2	Immediately following
	Scene 3	One o'clock in the morning
	Scene 4	A few minutes later

The play was also produced at the Spa Pavilion, Felixstowe, in June 1989 with the following cast:

Baron Von Frankenstein	Michael Downing
Ygor	Ian Taylor
The Monster	Daniel Lambert
Frau Lurker	Ann Heyes
Baroness Von Frankenstein	Helen Allen
Harry Talbot	Paul Holden
Countess Ilona Bathory	Janice Greenwood
The Phantom of the Opera	Peter Tarrant
Count Vlad Dracula	Martin Downing
Isabel Channing	Victoria Potter

The play was directed by Martin Downing

Sound Manager (London)	Nick Jones
Lighting Manager (London and Felixstowe)	Arran McKnight
Sound Manager (Felixstowe)	Cai Dominic
Costumes by Michael Downing	

To Meta and Minnie McKinley——two wonderful people—for their unstinting support and great kindness over the many years.

Also to Trevor Ryder who provided the inspiration for the script.

And to the original actors who overcame all obstacles to stage this play so successfully!

With love—Martin

CHARACTERS

Baron Victor Von Frankenstein, a scientist
Baroness Elisabeth Von Frankenstein, his wife
Ygor, his assistant
Frau Lurker, his housekeeper
The Monster, his creation
Harry Talbot, a werewolf
Countess Ilona Bathory, the Queen of Vampires
The Phantom of the Opera, the Terror of Paris
Count Vlad Dracula, the King of Vampires
Isabel Channing, the Phantom's Protegée

CHARACTER DESCRIPTIONS

Baron Victor Von Frankenstein is about thirty-five years old. He is of clean cut appearance and speaks forcefully. An extrovert and emotional day-dreamer.

Ygor can be played at any age. He is a hunchback, ugly and speaks and shambles like Charles Laughton's Quasimodo. He is scruffy in appearance and extrovert and eccentric in manner.

The Monster resembles the "Creature" as played by Boris Karloff. He is of indeterminate age and appears to be the most stupid and pathetic being imaginable. He wears ill-fitting clothes and moves clumsily.

Frau Lurker is about sixty-five and has a dour and menacing manner. She speaks tersely with a harsh German accent and marches rather than walks. She wears unrelieved black. (Can be played by a man.)

Baroness Elisabeth Von Frankenstein is twenty-seven years old, very attractive, but diffident, bored and outspoken. Castle Frankenstein is not her idea of home.

Harry Talbot is a good looking if somewhat dejected American in his early thirties. He is obviously a loner but is capable of arousing sympathy. He has to be able to dance.

Countess Ilona Bathory appears to be in her late thirties and is both attractive and stylishly dressed. Her manner is usually restrained, but there are moments when her true passions are revealed. She speaks with a mid-European accent. She should be able to dance.

The Phantom of the Opera is about forty, but it is hard to tell since his face is almost entirely concealed by a mask. He is French and his mood varies from one of menace to that of the dispirited romantic.

Count Vlad Dracula appears to be in his mid-forties. He speaks with a Romanian accent and his appearance is suave yet sinister. His manner varies between dejection and ferocity, but at all times he should appear formid-able. He should be able to dance.

Isabel Channing is an American in her early twenties. She is attractive but her manner is abrasive. Like most of the other characters she is a total extrovert. She is also a dancer.

Costume suggestions follow at the end of the text.

It is important to remember that this play is a comedy-horror. Therefore the sinister characters should play their parts with real malevolence at times, to supply the right balance in the action

ACT I

SCENE 1

The Great Hall at Castle Frankenstein. Shortly before 7 p.m. High stone walls form the framework and set into these up R and up L are two enormous gothic windows which overlook a grim mountainous landscape. Surmounting the windows are carved wooden pelmets which support floor length curtains with tapestry tie-backs. Between the windows is a massive stone fireplace, heavily carved, above which is the Frankenstein coat of arms: a shield divided into quarters which contain a head, an arm, a leg and a saw respectively. The shield is surmounted by an ornate crest, while below is emblazoned the motto: NICE WORK IF YOU CAN GET IT. Arranged on top of the mantelpiece are two silver candelabra and various preserving jars containing eyeballs, brains etc. The focal point is a mounted human skull. A bell-rope hangs to the right of the fireplace

A set of double doors open off the Hall up R, giving access to the castle grounds. A single door opens off down L. This leads to other reception rooms and the kitchen. Up L is a stone staircase with balustrade which leads to the bedrooms. Down R, set into the wall, is a secret panel which opens off the Hall. Above this panel stands a small table; below it is a library chair. There is a similar chair below the door down L. Slightly to the R of centre stands an ornate baronial chair and a side-table. To the L of centre is an old-fashioned sofa and there is another table against the wall L. Two more library chairs stand on either side of the fireplace

The central area of the Hall floor is covered by a worn carpet. There are animal heads over the doors and shields, maces and axes on the walls. Two large iron candleholders stand at the foot of the staircase and behind the baronial chair respectively. The table R supports an oil lamp; the one L a pile of books

To the sound of menacing music the CURTAIN *rises to reveal the Hall as a scene of fading daylight and long shadows. The oil lamp and the candleholders have been lit, but the curtains have not yet been drawn*

Baron Victor Von Frankenstein, wearing a laboratory coat over his other clothes is standing centre. He is holding a conical flask containing powder and is being watched avidly by his hunchback assistant, Ygor

Baron (*passionately*) Since man first emerged from the mists of ignorance and realized his identity he has had but *one* ambition: to be recognized, to be remembered—to be *renowned*!

Ygor That's *three*, Master.

Baron Shut up! Yes—man has always craved fame. Fame for an achievement unsurpassed in the history of his species—an achievement which will
set him on a pinnacle above his peers! (*His voice increases in volume*) Once
there he can gaze down in triumph at all those who scoffed, at all who
jeered and mocked, hurling back their petty insults certain he has the
forces of truth and experience on his side!

Ygor Duh—*why*?

Baron Because men love to gloat. And tonight *I*, Baron Victor Von
Frankenstein, have every *right* to gloat!

Ygor (*wide-eyed*) You mean—?

Baron *Yes*, Ygor—we are about to conduct the *final* experiment!

Ygor Oh, Master!

Baron And with it comes my *success*. My *long-awaited* success. My "never
mind the thousands of previous cock-ups, this is *it*!" success! Did you give
Frau Lurker my note?

Ygor Yes, Master, and all is prepared.

Baron Excellent! (*He moves to put the flask on the table next to the baronial
chair*)

The door down L *opens to admit the Monster, who shuffles in carrying a
beaker full of hot water*

(*Imperiously*) Bring that here, carefully.

The Monster moves clumsily, spilling some of the liquid

I said *carefully*! (*To Ygor*) Why doesn't he listen?

Ygor Because he's thick, Master.

Baron (*scathingly*) He's not the only one! Good God, if I'd known scientific
progress depended on the assistance of six-foot cabbages and half-wit
hunchbacks I'd have stayed a biology teacher!

The Monster hands him the beaker

Let's get on with the experiment.

Ygor Yes, Master!

*The Baron picks up the flask from the table and, with the beaker in his other
hand, moves downstage*

Baron Tonight, my faithful morons, you are going to witness a scientific
marvel comparable to the feat performed by our *Creator* when he
populated the primeval oceans with the tiny senseless amoeba which were
our ancestors—and your *parents*, Ygor!

Ygor Duh?

Baron *I*, by adding the contents of this beaker to that flask, am going to
achieve a *similar* triumph. A triumph which will secure me an everlasting
place in the Hall of Fame! Watch, dimwits, as I, Victor Von Frankenstein,
create *LIFE*!!

*Lightning flashes vividly as he pours the liquid into the flask. Ygor and the
Monster look terrified. Thunder rolls as he then raises the flask above his head*

(*Triumphantly*) I have *succeeded*! See! See for yourselves! Creatures that *move*—creatures that *breathe*—creatures that LIVE!! (*He hands the flask to Ygor and moves to place the beaker on the table*)

Ygor (*peering into the flask, bemused*) They're *croutons*, Master.

Baron What?

Ygor Croutons. You've just created *Minestrone soup*—with *croutons*!

Baron (*warily*) How do you *know*?

Ygor (*pointing*) That's a *noodle*—and there's a bit of *cabbage*, and all those *square* things . . .

Baron Rubbish!

Ygor A lot of folks say that, but it's still pretty popular! (*He drinks from the flask, smacking his lips*)

Baron (*resigned*) Damn! I can't fool anyone any more. Not even a *cretin*.

Ygor A *partial* cretin, Master. D'you want any of this? It's rather yummy!

Baron (*shuddering*) *No*. I can't stand the way those croutons bob against my lips.

Ygor (*mischievously*) As if they were *alive*, Master?

Baron Shut up!

Ygor grins and continues slurping from the flask

The door DL *opens to admit Frau Lurker. She strides in clutching a bloodstained meat cleaver*

Everyone recoils

Frau Lurker Herr Baron, I have seen to the visitors!

Baron (*alarmed*) Frau Lurker, you haven't—!

Frau Lurker *Ja*! We now have enough meat for dinner. Come—*see*!

Baron (*grimacing*) No thanks.

Frau Lurker There is not much blood *this* time.

Baron How come?

Ygor The cow was already *dead*, Master.

Baron (*to Frau Lurker*) You could still have let the *butcher* carve it up!

Frau Lurker (*fiercely*) He is too mean with his cuts! A steak from him would not feed a *puppy*! *I* am much more generous . . . (*Brandishing the cleaver*) A chop is a *chop*! Your guests tonight, Herr Baron, will not have to firk through the vegetables to *locate* their meat . . . It will sit there *proudly* for all the world to *admire*!

Ygor (*slyly*) As large as *life*, Master.

Baron Shut up! (*Drily*) You reassure me, Frau Lurker. What is it to be? Sirloin? T-bone?

Frau Lurker (*thumping Ygor on the rear*) Rump! Und *lots of it*!

Ygor Oi! Don't get fresh!

The Baron looks disgusted

The doors UR *open to admit the Baroness Von Frankenstein. She is folding a wet umbrella and looks distinctly annoyed*

Baron Ah, Elisabeth, my dear. Did you enjoy your walk?

Baroness Are you *serious*? The heavens opened and I got soaked! Frau Lurker, has the sun *ever* shown its face in this part of the world?

Frau Lurker (*dourly*) Nein. It is always chucking it down!

Ygor (*brightly*) It's a nice day when it snows!

Baroness (*drily*) I'm sure. (*Urgently*) Victor, I can't bear another minute in this dismal, damp, dark, ~~God-forsaken~~ unbearable old dump! You have to take me away—*now*!

Baron (*puzzled*) But you said the castle had charm.

Baroness That was *Windsor*! *This* place is the absolute pits!

Ygor *I* think it's cosy.

Baroness *You* would! (*Pleading*) Victor, we *must* leave. I insist.

Baron But dearest—my *experiments*.

Baroness *What* experiments? You haven't done anything in the least useful since we arrived!

Baron That's not true. I've made *incredible* advances!

Baroness So has the bank manager—but for *what*?

Baron (*pointing to the Monster*) I made *him*!

Baroness You call *that* an achievement?

Baron Well, not precisely—but it's a start.

Baroness Ha!

Ygor (*gesturing to the Baron*) He makes a good Cup-A-Soup!

Baron Shut up!

Frau Lurker (*sharply*) What about the house plants? *Those* were a success.

Baron (*proudly*) Undeniably!

Baroness (*dryly*) Victor, when I told you that plants enjoy being talked to I wasn't asking you to invent a fertilizer which gave them the ability to *talk back*!

Baron So?

Baroness All they do *now* is ~~bitch about~~ criticize my appearance! It's infuriating!

Baron It's still a *success*!

Baroness (*patiently*) There's more to life than success or fame or whatever else is driving you along the path you've taken, Victor. There are other things which can make a person happy. Normal, everyday things like comfort, companionship—*romance*!

Ygor Yuck!

All Shut up!

Baroness (*to the Baron*) Do you understand?

Baron (*gruffly*) Yes, but there's no *challenge* in those things.

Baroness (*impatiently*) You *don't* understand. Oh, Victor—!

The castle clock strikes seven o'clock

Ygor (*excited*) The clock! The clock!

Baron (*sharply*) Listen to me—all of you. Our *guests* will be arriving very shortly.

Frau Lurker (*abruptly*) Und how long will they *stay*?

Baron Overnight.

There is a stunned silence

Ygor But Master—no-one *ever* stays overnight!
Baroness Not here.
Frau Lurker Not if they *know* us!
Baroness It's impossible! The bathroom gets crowded enough as it is!
Baron I'm sorry, Elisabeth—but it's a *must*. For reasons of anonymity and
  safety they have to spend the night in the *castle*.
Baroness But *why*?
Baron (*awkwardly*) These people have ... *problems*.
Baroness (*sharply*) Yes—*meanness* and *cheek*!
Baron (*ignoring her*) And they want to ask my *scientific advice*.

There is much falling about. The Baron looks annoyed

  Quiet! It's behaviour like that which gives a scientist a bad name!
  Elisabeth—I suggest that you and I go and get changed. Ygor—
Ygor Yes, Master?
Baron Help Frau Lurker to make the beds.

  The Baron and the Baroness exit up the staircase

Frau Lurker (*to Ygor, imperatively*) I will get the hammer—*you* get the
  nails ... (*Pointing to the Monster*) We will use *him* as a work-bench!
  Schnell! Schnell!

  Frau Lurker exits DL

Ygor salutes nervously as she goes then turns to the Monster

Ygor Oi—Einstein! (*Pointing to the door*) Mush!

  The Monster shambles out and Ygor follows him

*A motor-bike is heard arriving outside the castle. It stops and then footsteps
are heard approaching* UR. *The castle doorbell tolls loudly*

  Ygor enters DL

Ygor (*excitedly*) The bells! The bells! (*He lurches across to the doors* UR, *and
  opens them in a deliberately sinister fashion. Leering offstage*) Y-e-s-s?
Talbot (*off*) I've come to see Baron Von Frankenstein ... Hope I've got the
  right place?
Ygor (*stepping back*) Y-e-s-s! *Do* come in ... The Master is expecting you.
Talbot (*off*) Great!

  *Talbot steps into the room carrying a rucksack and a crash-helmet. He
  stares at his surroundings*

Ygor closes the door

Ygor (*over Talbot's shoulder*) You must be—(*ducking under his arm to look
  at the rucksack label*) Mr Talbot ...
Talbot (*startled by Ygor's manoeuvres*) That's right. You know me?
Ygor Not exactly—but your *fist* rings a bell! Heh, heh, heh!
Talbot (*drily*) A wise-guy, huh?
Ygor I like to think so ... But I could be wrong.

Talbot Where's the Baron?

Ygor Upstairs, sir—dressing for dinner. He'll be down in a moment.

Talbot Fine. D'you mind if I make myself comfortable?

Ygor You can try! (*Moving to the staircase*) I'll see if your room's free.

Talbot (*puzzled*) You've chucked someone out?

Ygor (*grinning*) Not some*one*, sir . . . Some *rats*!

Talbot (*with feeling*) They'd better not come back! (*He puts his rucksack and crash-helmet on the sofa*)

Ygor *You* certainly won't . . . Heh, heh!

Ygor exits, chuckling

The door DL *opens and Frau Lurker enters followed by the Monster, who is carrying a tray with a sherry decanter and glasses*

She stops short when she sees Talbot and the Monster almost falls over her

Frau Lurker (*sharply*) Who are you?

Talbot The name's Harry Talbot. And you're—?

Frau Lurker Never mind! Why are you here?

Talbot I've come to see the Baron.

Frau Lurker (*hissing*) You are a fool!

Talbot Hey?

Frau Lurker (*advancing and gripping his arm*) You should not have come here! It is not *safe*! This castle is evil—*evil*! Terrible things have happened here—things you cannot possibly *imagine*!

Talbot (*wincing under the pressure of her grip*) Such as?

Frau Lurker (*eagerly, having first peered round the room*) There was a young man, handsome und *sexy* like you, who came here a year ago. He was looking for a wild flower . . .

Talbot A *pansy*, huh?

Frau Lurker *Nein*—the Carpathian Rock Rose. *He* was foolish enough to stay here. (*With feeling*) Und in the *night*—(*shuddering*)—you have never heard such *screams*! They were terrible—*terrible*! (*Chuckling*) Well worth staying up for . . . In the morning we found him lying outside on the drive, his clothes torn und drenched in *blood*! Und his *face*—(*wide-eyed*)—*Gott in Himmel*, I cannot describe it even *now*!

Talbot Why not?

Frau Lurker (*with relish*) Something had run off with his *head*!!

Talbot grimaces. She grips his arm even more tightly

So, young man, you must leave at once—before it is too late!

Talbot But I've only just got here!

Frau Lurker releases his arm which he rubs

Frau Lurker You will not listen? So be it. No-one can say I did not *warn* you. (*Fiercely*) But remember this, my fine young friend—in Castle Frankenstein NO-ONE CAN HEAR YOU SCREAM!

Talbot You just said you could!

Frau Lurker (*maniacally*) That was before we bought the sleeping pills!

She turns laughing wildly, and marches out of the door DL

Talbot stares after her shaking his head

Ygor re-enters on the staircase

Ygor (*sepulchrally*) The Master!

The Baron comes down the staircase buttoning his dinner jacket

He extends a hand to Talbot who shakes it

Baron Welcome to Castle Frankenstein, Mr Talbot. You had a pleasant journey, I trust? (*He gestures for Ygor to pour two glasses of sherry*)

Talbot Sure. But tell me, Baron—where the hell did you get your staff? They're *weird*!

Baron A little odd, perhaps—but they're good souls and accept pitiful wages.

Ygor scowls behind his back

Why? Have they done something to offend you?

Talbot Oh, no. One of them just tried to scare the pants off me, that's all!

Baron (*smiling*) That would be Frau Lurker, our Housekeeper and resident Valkyrie. She has a rather colourful turn of phrase. Don't let it worry you.

Ygor hands them both sherry during the exchange and then goes to lurk upstage. The Baron and Talbot both sit

Talbot I won't. (*Dourly*) I've more important things on my mind. As *you* know.

Baron Indeed—and I trust I'm able to help you, Mr Talbot.

Talbot So do I.

The Baron takes a letter from his pocket and opens it

Baron According to your letter you are suffering from an affliction which has been baffling medical science for years . . .

Talbot (*grimly*) Yeah. I'm not like other men!

Baron This might lead to a variety of assumptions, some of which are real *eye-openers*, but fortunately your last paragraph gave rise to a *different* explanation and, I may add, a great sigh of relief on my part! On certain nights each month—

Talbot (*with feeling*) When the moon is full—

Baron And the rest of mankind is asleep—

Talbot I turn into a *wolf*!

There is a dramatic chord to which they all react and then the Baron folds the letter and puts it away

Baron Exactly.

The Baron and Ygor exchange glances and then fall about laughing

Talbot (*sharply*) What's so funny?

Baron (*wiping his eyes*) Oh nothing, nothing ... (*To Ygor*) It's a gem!
   Priceless!
Ygor A real howler, Master!

There is more falling about

Talbot (*angrily*) If this is the way you're going to treat me, I'm leavin'!
Baron (*with difficulty*) I'm sorry, Mr Talbot—I didn't mean to be heartless
   ... It's just that—hoo, hoo!
Talbot (*snarling savagely*) It's no joke!
Baron (*sobering*) No, no—I'm sure it isn't. Not for *you*, at least.
Talbot (*grimly*) Right!

The Baron gestures for Ygor to leave the Hall

   Ygor exits DL, *grinning broadly*

Baron (*to Talbot*) How did you come by such a ... problem?
Talbot Real easy! (*Moving centre, he declaims the following with feeling*)

> A gypsy once told me— when I was in short pants—"Son,
> A wolf's gonna nip you, when you are out hikin',
> But once that Band-Aid's undone
> You'll wind up a *fuzz-face*, a four-legged thing,
> Who only can *yelp* an' *howl* in the night!

Baron Indeed?
Talbot

> Well, she was just a crazy an' a rollin' drunk,
> Smellin' like she'd been with some funky old skunk!
> I told her to move her face fast or I'd sock it—
> That's *not* what I wanted to hear!
>
> But I got bit when I was twenty, see.
> Went an' told the gypsy, but she *freaked* on me!
> "Take that bite back to the place where you got it!
> *I don't want no werewolf in here*!!"
>
> When I reached home about half-past three
> I looked in the mirror an' what did I *see*?
> *Fur, fangs an' all*—boy, had I *got* it!
> I sure was a *stranger* to me!
>
> Well, you never do get nothin' bein' a *hairy* guy!
> I gotta change my ways, an' you wanna know why?
> Levis ain't neat with a *tail* when you got it—
> An' girls hate a guy with *long ears*!!
>
> Man, once, you're half a wolf you find that life sure ain't
>   fair—
> 'Cos when your fists are *paws* you've no friends *anywhere*!
> I wanna tell you somethin'—I won't tell you no lies—
> *Werewolves* are the only guys who *never* get by! Huh!

Werewolves sure *worry!*
Werewolves sure get the *blues!!*

Baron Fascinating!

Talbot (*urgently*) You know what I'm talkin' about—don't you?

Baron (*curious*) Yes, but when you become a wolf do you know what's *happened* to you? Are you still Harry Talbot *inside?*

Talbot (*grimly*) Sure! 'Cept I can't stop myself doin', well, *doggy* things . . . Like chasin' cats, sniffin' trees, howlin' at Kate Bush records an' chewin' up the odd tramp! I try—but I *can't!* It's a goddamn *nightmare*, believe me! (*He falls to his knees in despair*)

Baron (*moving to pat his head*) I *do*, boy. There are times when *all* of us do things beyond our control—things we regret but can't *help* doing . . . As if we were manipulated by another being inside us—(*with rising volume*)— another *mind*, another *intelligence*, another *genius!*

Talbot looks wary, but the Baron controls his passion

Fortunately those who are so afflicted are usually relegated to institutions for the *hopelessly insane!*

Talbot (*rising, urgently*) You're not sayin' that I—?

Baron No, no. I'll do my best to help you solve your problem, Mr Talbot. It may be *tricky*—but not impossible . . .

Talbot But how soon can you come up with an answer? I mean, there's a full moon tonight and it's a dead cert . . .

Baron I'll start work on an antidote right away. But just in case there's a set-back—

Talbot Oh hell!

Baron Wear loose clothes and make sure there's a lead handy . . . (*He pulls the bell-rope and a bell rings off* L)

Talbot Why?

Baron Then someone can take you for a walk!

Talbot (*glumly*) Fine!

The door DL *opens and Ygor gallops in*

Ygor (*excitedly*) The bells! The bells!

Talbot (*to the Baron*) Where did you get *him?*

Baron Paris, nineteen eighty. He was hanging round Notre Dame Cathedral . . . *Literally!* Ygor—

Ygor Yes, Master?

Baron Show Mr Talbot to his room.

Ygor Certainly. (*Gesturing to the staircase*) This way, sir . . . (*As they move*) You'll find it a very *nice* kennel!

Baron (*sharply*) Ygor! The Dr Pavlov Suite!

Ygor (*grinning*) Sorry, Master!

Ygor and Talbot exit, Talbot taking his rucksack and crash-helmet with him

The Baron, looking perplexed, goes to draw the curtains UR

The Baroness enters from the staircase, casting a glance behind her. She is now wearing evening dress

Baroness (*drawing the curtains* UL) Was that the first of your guests, Victor?
Baron Yes, dear. His name's Harry Talbot.
Baroness Quite handsome, from what I've glimpsed.
Baron If you say so.
Baroness (*musing*) D'you think he's a *wolf*?
Baron (*drily*) Not at the moment.

The Baroness moves DL

Darling, don't go into the dining-room just yet.
Baroness Why not?
Baron Frau Lurker's removing the last of the *geraniums*.
Baroness One nagging plant I can cope with!
Baron (*firmly*) Not that one. It also *spits* and makes *obscene suggestions*!
Baroness (*wryly*) Oh—*nice*!

The Baroness exits DL

The Baron replaces the sherry glasses on the Monster's tray, makes a face at him but gets no reaction. He shrugs

The Baron exits DL

A second later we hear a carriage arriving off R. *The carriage door opens and closes and then footsteps approach the main doors. There is a sudden pounding off* R

The Monster moans as if trying to attract attention and then moves inadequately round in a circle. The bell sounds

Ygor bounds in from the staircase

Ygor (*excitedly*) The bells! The—(*he collides with the Monster*) Watch where you're going!

The Monster mumbles irritably

And don't answer back!

The bell sounds again

Keep your knickers on . . . ! (*He opens the doors and leers off*) Wel-come to Castle Frankenstein!

Countess Bathory glides through the door

Ygor stares at her appreciatively

Countess Good—I was not sure this was the correct destination.

Frau Lurker enters DL

I must now dismiss my driver.
Frau Lurker (*forcefully*) Don't! Leave *now*—while you still have the chance!
Countess I beg your pardon?

Frau Lurker Those who enter Castle Frankenstein never live *long*. Their fate is sealed once that door closes behind them! You cannot imagine the *horror* which awaits you if you remain!

Countess (*unmoved*) I will risk it. I have nothing to lose. (*Calling off*) Driver, you may leave!

She steps further into the Hall and Ygor shuts the doors

Frau Lurker You will not listen? So be it! But hear *this* ... There was a young woman, very attractive und *sickeningly stylish* like you, who visited this castle a month ago. *She* was foolish enough to stay here ... (*Shuddering*) Und in the *night*—

Countess You heard *terrible screams*?

Ygor We heard nothing!

Frau Lurker (*irritably*) But in the *morning*—

Countess You found her *dead*?

Frau Lurker (*folding her arms, sharply*) Who is doing the frightening? *Me or you?*

Ygor
Countess } (*together; startled*) You.

Frau Lurker Good! (*Resuming her former manner*) In the *morning* we could not find a trace of her! No hair, no blood—*nothing*! She had vanished—*into thin air*!

Ygor (*blithely*) And so had half the *silver*!

Frau Lurker (*furious*) Dumkopf! (*She clouts him*) You have *ruined* my story!

Ygor (*cowering*) Sorry! Sorry! Don't *hit* me!

Countess Well—at least *she* survived.

Frau Lurker (*petulantly*) She was an *exception*. It must have been an off-night. But as for *you*—tonight, here in this house of evil, you will be AFRAID! You will be VERY AFRAID!!

The Countess shrugs and Frau Lurker grabs Ygor by the scruff of the neck and marches him towards the door DL

(*Fiercely to Ygor*) Und so will *you* if you spoil any more stories!

The Baron enters as they reach the door

Ygor (*half-strangled*) The Master!

Ygor and Frau Lurker exit

The Baron approaches the Countess, who extends her hand

Baron Countess Bathory? (*Kissing her hand*) I am delighted to have you as my guest.

Countess And I am delighted to be here, my dear Baron.

Baron Would you care for sherry?

Countess Thank you.

The Baron pours two glasses

But tell me, your *staff*—where did you acquire such *strange* domestics?

Baron Oh—here and there. You find them interesting?

Countess I find them *weird*! (*Shrugging*) But that is not so very unusual. In my circle of acquaintances there are a great many odd personalities. Perhaps not *quite* as odd as the two I have just encountered—but odd nevertheless.

Baron (*handing her a glass*) Do you happen to know a Mr Talbot?

Countess (*sitting on the sofa*) I have heard his name mentioned. Usually in the context of a joke! He is the young man who has the misfortune of being a werewolf?

Baron That is so. (*Musing*) His is a strange tale.

Countess (*drily*) And a *bushy* one, I should think.

Baron What? Er—quite! He is *also* my guest this evening.

Countess I am intrigued. He has come, as *I* have, to seek your advice?

Baron Yes. But the two problems are very different. *He* is a werewolf—

Countess Whereas *I*, dear Baron, am a *vampire*!

There is a dramatic chord to which they both react

Baron So I understand.

Countess But we have *one* area of common ground, Mr Talbot and I.

Baron And what is that?

Countess (*with feeling*) The *night*! The scene of our strange and unfortunate existence. While all others rest *we* are forced to roam the darkened streets like characters in a macabre puppet show, acting out a grim pageant for an audience of shadows!

Baron (*bemused*) You have played the Palladium?

Countess No.

Baron (*blithely*) My misunderstanding. But you have friends, surely?

Countess Friends?

Baron Other *vampires*.

Countess (*passionately*) Such *bores*, dear Baron! Pale, lifeless creatures, whose only topic of conversation is the merit of one blood group over another! (*Mimicking*) "Have you tried Sloane Ranger Rhesus Positive?". "Yes, but darling, *I* prefer a jugular of Young Urban Professional AB anyday!" (*Bitterly*) And the *zombies*! Have you ever met one?

Baron (*wryly*) I've taught a few!

Countess I mean the *real* zombies—victims of the Filofax cult who inhabit the wine bars of the inner cities and who constantly exhort me and my kind to buy Beaujolais Nouveau and dance to Dire Straits! They are a real *joy*, I assure you.

Baron And so—what do you want me to do?

Countess (*urgently*) I want you to help me escape this hellish existence! I *must* escape—before continual exposure to the inanity and predictability of the Living Dead results in my becoming totally and unutterably *morbid*! (*Pleading*) Do you *understand*?

Baron I do. And you have my assurance that I will do everything in my power to aid you, Countess. If not—(*bravely*)—I will hang myself from the nearest tree!

Countess I trust that will not be necessary.
Baron So do I. I should hate to deprive mankind of my genius!
Countess But do you really think—?
Baron That I would be *missed*? Certainly!
Countess No—are you able to devise me an antidote?
Baron (*ringing the bell*) I feel sure of it.
Countess God bless you, Baron!
Baron (*wryly*) I truly hope he will!

Ygor gallops in from DL

Ygor (*excitedly*) The bells! The—
Baron Shut up!
Ygor Sorry, Master!
Baron Show the Countess to the Lugosi Suite.
Ygor (*saluting grotesquely*) Yes, sir!
Countess And I will give you a guinea if you transport my luggage from the doorstep.
Ygor Fangs!
Baron Ygor!
Ygor (*whining*) Sorry again, Master!

Ygor escorts the Countess up the staircase

The Baroness enters from DL

Baroness (*staring after the Countess*) I assume that was another of your guests . . . ?
Baron Yes, dear. The Countess Ilona Bathory.
Baroness (*unimpressed*) Really.
Baron (*wryly*) Rather attractive—from what I've glimpsed.
Baroness (*diffidently*) If you say so . . . I'd say she was a vamp . . .
Baron (*rubbing his hands*) Most definitely!
Baroness (*angrily*) Oh, Victor!

The Baroness exits haughtily DL

The Baron grins after her and then takes his glass back to the Monster

Baron Same again, barman!

The Monster growls

Hey, who's boss here?

The Monster mutters

That's more like it! (*He refills his glass*) if you're not careful, I'll dismember you! You'll be back in your graves before you know it!

The Baron knocks back the sherry as the Monster moans in a pleading fashion

(*Firmly*) Well then—behave yourself!

The Baron exits DL

The Monster shuffles miserably

The Lights fade to a black-out

SCENE 2

Ten minutes later

When the Lights come up the Monster is still on stage, dozing. Suddenly there is a terrific gust of wind and the doors UR fly open. The Monster wakes with a start and watches, terrified, as the grim figure of The Phantom Of The Opera slinks into the Hall. He prowls round and then approaches the Monster, who moans. Producing a letter, The Phantom places it on the tray and then gibbers at the Monster who emits a terrified yell

The Phantom then moves quickly DR and disappears into the wall using the secret panel

 A second later the Baron, the Baroness, Frau Lurker and Ygor rush in from DL

Ygor (*excited*) A scream! A scream!
Baroness What is it? What's happened?
Frau Lurker (*seeing the Monster's fear*) Gott in Himmel—it's that dumkopf Monster!

The Monster moans frantically

Baroness Slow down, you stupid creature!
Frau Lurker We can't understand you!
Ygor So what's new?
Baron Shut up and watch his lips ...

The Monster moans again

Frau Lurker What is he saying?
Baron (*nonplussed*) He's just seen a *ghost*!
Ygor Which one?
Baron Something horrible—something unspeakable! (*To Ygor*) *You* weren't in here, were you?
Ygor (*affronted*) Master!

The Monster continues to moan

Baroness (*pointing DR*) He says it went into the wall—over there!

They all look at the wall, the Monster and then at the sherry decanter

All (*nodding*) He's been at the sherry!

The Monster shakes his head furiously but they ignore him. The Baron suddenly sees the letter on the tray

Baron Hey! What's this?

Ygor Looks like a letter, Master.

Baron (*drily*) Ygor, are you as stupid as you *look*—or do you look more stupid than you *are*?

Ygor (*scratching his head*) Duh ... (*Brightly*) I'm as stupid as I look, Master!

Baron Exactly!

Baroness (*reaching for the letter*) Let's see what it says.

Frau Lurker (*grabbing*) Let me!

Ygor No—*me*!

Baron (*wresting it away from them*) Please—it's not a Pools win!

The others listen avidly as he reads aloud

"Baron, I am sending you a note of the most malevolent nature detailing how you are to conduct this evening's events. Pay close attention to my instructions if you value your life." (*Wide-eyed*) What the—?!

Organ music plays as the voice of The Phantom takes over and everyone stares above and around them, puzzled

Phantom (*off*) That delight of the Paris stage, Mam'selle Isabel Channing will visit you tonight and I am anxious that you do not meddle with 'er singing career. Be prepared for something nasty should you try to take my place!

The voice and music fade out

Baroness Who has dared to send this?

Baron Somebody with no *brain*!

They all look at Ygor

Ygor (*pleading*) It wasn't me, Master!

Baron Then who?

Frau Lurker (*pointing*) It is signed "P. O. O."

Baron Who the hell's *that*?

The Others Pooh!

Baron That's really *not* amusing!

Frau Lurker (*pointing to Ygor*) *He* said it!

Ygor No, I didn't!

Baroness Yes, you *did*!

Baron (*shouting*) Quiet, all of you!

There is a sudden pounding on the doors UR *and everyone looks terrified*

Ygor It's here!

Frau Lurker It is with us!

Baroness It's the ghost!

All Three It's *Pooh*!

Baroness I'm off!

The Baroness exits at top speed DL

Baron (*calling after her*) Don't be idiotic!

The pounding is repeated and the Baron looks nervous

Answer the door, Ygor— and try to control yourself. I'm just going to put this somewhere safe!

The Baron races off after the Baroness

Ygor advances towards the doors, trembling. Frau Lurker and the Monster look terrified

The pounding is repeated

Ygor If I die before I sleep, I pray the Lord my soul to keep! (*Opening the doors; timidly*) Welcome to Castle Fragglestein ... (*He jumps back, terrified, as:*)

Count Dracula steps across the threshhold. He is lit by an eerie light and looks totally sinister

Count (*deadly*) Good evening.

Ygor (*wide-eyed*) Yerk!

Count I am here to see your Master, the Baron. Where is he?

Ygor (*with difficulty*) Hiding—somewhere ... Do you *really* want to see him?

Count Yes!

Ygor (*dismally*) I had a hunch you might!

Frau Lurker (*advancing*) You don't know what you're *asking, mein Herr.*

Count I *do.*

Frau Lurker You *don't.* If you only knew this place as *we* do you would never dare pop in for a *chat*! This house is cursed—CURSED!

Count (*drily*) Really?

Frau Lurker (*nodding*) Ja! There was a man, tall, strong und handsome like you—only he wasn't so *pale*—who came here a week ago. He was a *poet.*

Count A romantic?

Frau Lurker (*coyly*) He blew me a kiss! Anyway, he stayed for the night to complete his latest poem.

Count Odd.

Frau Lurker Nein—an ode. Und he wanted an atmospheric room to write in. (*With feeling*) We gave him the *Bloody Tower*! It is *very* atmospheric!

Count In what way?

Ygor It's freezing, draughty and the roof leaks!

Count Did he finish the poem?

Frau Lurker Nein—he never had the chance! In the morning, when I pretended to take him breakfast, I opened the door und,—oh, mein Herr, it was horrible—*horrible*! That poor man ...

Count (*impatiently*) Well?

Ygor He was—

Frau Lurker (*fiercely*) Shut up! (*To the Count*) He was lying upon the bed, his body *twisted,* und his *face*—I have never seen such *terror*!

Ygor (*drily*) True.

Frau Lurker gives Ygor a filthy look and he recoils

Count He was *dead*?

Frau Lurker (*irritably*) Of course—but that's not important ... It was *how* he died! (*Wide-eyed*) He had choked on his *manuscript*! Something had made him *eat his own words*!!

Count (*shrugging*) It sounds like poetic justice!

Frau Lurker It is *proof*, mein Herr. Proof that no-one who enters Castle Frankenstein ever leaves *alive*!

Count (*surveying them*) Well, *I* have nothing to fear. I am already *dead*!

There is a dramatic chord to which they all react

Frau Lurker
Ygor } (*together*) (*open-mouthed*) Eh?

Count (*grimly*) So cut the Gruesome Twosome act and get back to the kitchen. Now!!

Ygor (*terrified*) Yes, sir!

Frau Lurker (*terrified*) At once, mein Herr!

They both rush to the door DL

Ygor (*to Frau Lurker*) He's bad!

Frau Lurker He's a bad man!

Ygor
Frau Lurker } (*together; nodding*) He's a *very* bad man!

Count (*sotto voce*) *Weird*!

The Baron enters

Ygor and Frau Lurker collide with the Baron as they make for the exit

Ygor (*over his shoulder*) The Master—God help him!

Ygor and Frau Lurker exit

Count Good evening, Herr Baron

Baron (*startled*) Good evening ... You must be—(*perplexed*) Forgive me, but are you *Pooh*?

Count I beg your pardon?

There is an amused chuckle from The Phantom offstage

Baron (*quickly*) No, of course not! You are ... You're—

Count I am Count Dracula.

Baron (*choking*) Count ... *Dracula*?

Count That is what I said.

Baron (*with feeling*) Good God!

Count (*wincing*) Please—refrain from blasphemy if you will. I have strong religious principles.

Baron (*wryly*) I never would have guessed!

Count I have come here—albeit unexpectedly—to consult you on a personal matter. I crave your advice.

Baron So long as that's all.

Count Do not wet yourself. I have already partaken of a quick bite.

Baron (*alarmed*) Not *here*?

Count No—in the village. The Slavonic equivalent of a Spud-U-Like. Total stodge—but it will suffice.

Baron Thank God!

Count (*raising a finger*) Herr Baron!

Baron Sorry. Would you like a sherry? Or can't you drink—

Count (*quickly*) Wine? Not only a cliché but a totally misplaced notion. I drink like a fish. Make it a large one.

Baron Certainly. (*He goes over to the Monster and pours two glasses*)

Count (*watching him*) Your drinks trolley has a most unique design ... Obtained from Habitat?

Baron Several locations, actually. It was a do-it-yourself job.

Count Indeed? Most impressive!

Baron (*returning with the drinks*) Thank you. It also serves as a coat stand and—with cunning attachments—a standard lamp!

Count Value For Money!

Baron (*sitting*) Now—how can I be of service to you, Count?

Count My problem concerns another of your guests.

Baron Mr Talbot?

Count Certainly not! I am not of that persuasion, and even if I were I could not cope with that young man. His shaggy dog stories are tedious beyond belief!

Baron Then who—?

Count (*passionately*) The Countess Ilona Bathory!

Baron Aaah.

Count I see you, too, have fallen for her charms.

Baron Not exactly. I was merely trying to sound intelligent. Carry on.

Count The Countess and I have known each other for many years. *Centuries*, in fact. During this time we became increasingly attracted to each other and finally, in the year eighteen forty-four, we became engaged.

Baron A hasty decision?

Count Far from it. We were, by then, mature in outlook and marriage seemed logical.

Baron Before or after the millenium?

Count We had not fixed a date. (*Sadly*) And now it seems we never will. Ilona has changed her mind!

Baron May I ask why?

Count Because she is bored with our decadent lifestyle—bored with the never-ending series of one-night stands which *I* particularly enjoy—bored with the dismal company of our kind ... (*With feeling*) Bored, in fact, with *me*—*me*, Count Vlad Dracula, a prince of the Magyar race, *revered* in my own time and a symbol of *terror* for countless generations thereafter! How is this *possible*?

Baron (*stifling a yawn*) It's hard to say ...

Count (*grimly*) It wasn't for *her*! Herr Baron, what am I to do?

Baron Forget you ever met?

Count (*bitterly*) I cannot! I have tried, but it is useless. She draws me like a magnet wherever she goes. That is why I am here tonight. I am under a *spell*, Herr Baron. A spell from which I cannot escape!

Baron Do you *want* to escape?

Count (*weakly*) I do not know ... To keep her I must change, which seems impossible, apart from becoming a *wolf* or a *bat*, which is limiting ... To leave her would be *torment*—that, too, is impossible ... *I* cannot reconcile such impossibilities. Can *you*?

Baron (*rising*) Having made a semi-human drinks trolley which doubles as a coat stand and a standard lamp, anything is possible! (*He tugs the bell-rope*)

Count If you succeed, Herr Baron, you will earn my everlasting gratitude!

Baron (*wryly*) A few *quid* wouldn't go amiss!

The Count bows and clicks his heels. The Baron smiles faintly

The door DL *opens and Ygor gallops in*

Ygor (*excited*) The bells The b ... b ... b ... (*He stops short, seeing the Count*)

Baron I presume you, too, would like to stay overnight, Count?

Count That is most kind. I welcome the offer.

Ygor (*under his breath*) *I* don't!

Count I shall not require a *bed*, however.

Baron (*drily*) Of course not.

Count Only the long box which is in my carriage outside. If someone will be so good as to transport it—?

Baron Certainly. Ygor—show the Count to the Crypt ... Suite and then attend to his—his—

Ygor *Coffin*, Master?

Baron Yes, well—do it!

Ygor (*to the Count, bravely*) I got a guinea for humping the last one. What's *yours* worth?

Count (*smiling*) A bedtime story?

Ygor (*recoiling*) I'll do it for *nix*!

Ygor exits up the staircase, keeping well ahead of the Count, who follows him

The Baron suddenly puts his hands to his head and paces round the room

Baron What have I got myself *into*?!

The wall panel slides open and The Phantom creeps out

He stalks the Baron, who is quite unaware of his presence. The Monster groans loudly

(*Turning to him*) What's wrong with you?

The Monster tries to indicate The Phantom with his head

Rubbish! There's no-one here. You're just imagining things!

As he speaks, The Phantom slips a letter into the pocket of the Baron's jacket, grins and then creeps back into the wall

The Monster groans yet again

(*Angrily*) I've *told* you—! (*He suddenly sees the letter*) Oh lord—what now?! (*He takes it out of his pocket, opens and reads it. Loudly; aghast*) This is damnable! *Damnable!*

Ygor, Frau Lurker and the Baroness rush in from DL

All What is it? What's wrong?
Baron Here's another letter!
The Others From *Pooh?*
Baron (*coldly*) From "P. O. O."! Listen ... "My dear Baron, my protegée, Mam'selle Isabel Channing is approaching your doorstep and I am anxious that you make her *very welcome ...*"

Organ music plays as the voice of The Phantom takes over and again everyone stares above and around them

Phantom (*off*) Be so good as to remember my previous instructions! Do not influence 'er in any way! I shall be watching your activities from various nooks and crannies in the masonry of this château. Should you disobey my commands a calamity beyond any adjective will occur! (*Suddenly*) Ugh! I've put my 'and on a slug!!

Organ music fades

Baron (*taking over*) "I remain, Baron, your malevolent servant, *P. O. O.*"
Baroness (*suddenly*) Ygor! He must be the one who wrote this!
Baron What on earth d'you mean?
Baroness The initials—are you blind?! "P. O. O." stands for Pathetic Obsequious Oddity!!
Baron Really? (*to the others*) Can you believe this?
Frau Lurker (*fervently*) Ja! Ja!
Ygor (*shaking his head*) No! No!
Baron (*abruptly*) This is insane ...

There is a sudden pounding on the doors UR *and everyone freezes*

That must be *her* ... !
Baroness Isabel Channing!
Ygor (*realizing*) Isabel? (*Excited*) *Is-a-bell!* Is-a-bell!
Baron Shut up and let her in ... (*Waving the letter*) But remember everyone—she's to be made very welcome!!

The Lights fade to black-out

SCENE 3

A minute later

When the Lights come up the pounding on the doors is repeated. Frau Lurker is now swinging her meat cleaver, the Baroness is polishing a dagger and the Baron is flexing a garrotte. They all look totally sinister

Baron (*deadly*) Open the door.
Ygor Yes, Master! (*He opens the door*)

Isabel Channing dances in to the sound of 30s show music. She is carrying a small suitcase which she thrusts at Ygor

Isabel finishes her routine and there is silence. Seeing the others' menacing demeanour, she is suddenly scared

Isabel *W-e-i-r-d!* Let me outta here!

Ygor slams the door shut and blocks her exit

Ygor (*leering*) You can't leave.
Isabel Why not?
Baron (*sounding like Boris Karloff*) Because, my dear Miss Channing, we want you to be our guest!
Isabel Huh?
Baroness (*sepulchrally*) We want to make you *welcome*!
Frau Lurker (*menacing*) We have *ways* of making you welcome!
Isabel (*recoiling*) Get away from me!
Ygor But we want to be your *friends* . . .
Baron So you will feel at home . . .
Frau Lurker Und spend the *night* with us!

The following lines are spoken with increasing momentum

Baroness This castle is incredibly *charming* . . .
Baron Not to mention *comfortable* . . .
Baroness It has *fairly hot* running water . . .
Baron *Superb* views . . .
Frau Lurker *All night entertainment* . . .
Baroness And there are Tupperware parties every other Tuesday!
Ygor You *will* like it here!
Frau Lurker You have *no choice*!
Isabel (*with difficulty*) It—sounds a dream . . . !
Baron (*smiling*) Then that's settled! Would you like a sherry?
Isabel (*dubiously*) Sure . . .
Baron Ygor—!

Ygor goes to the Monster and pours her a glass

Baroness (*inviting her to sit*) We understand you're a singer.
Isabel (*askance*) Who fed you that?
Baron Er—one of our other guests.

Isabel (*jumping to her feet*) Don't tell me he's here?!
Baroness Who?
Isabel That creepy old guy in the cloak and mask who keeps followin' me about!
Baron (*awkwardly*) We haven't actually *seen* him yet.

The Monster nods and moans

Isabel Consider yourselves lucky! Folks say he's got no *face*! *Gross!* Thank heaven he stays in the woodwork most of the time. (*Shouting at the walls*) So you found out where I was headin', you old crack-pot? Well, I hope you get *risin' damp*! (*To the Baron*) I thought I'd given him the slip, but you can't win 'em all!
Baron But why is he following you?
Isabel He's got the hots for me—that's why!
Baron We thought he might be your agent?
Isabel Are you kiddin'? He's just a busker—and he ain't even got a name!
Ygor (*handing her a glass of sherry*) Isn't it Pooh?
Isabel What? No, handsome—"P. O. O." 's how he signs himself, that's all. It stands for *Phantom of the Opera* ... (*Wryly*) What a poser!

There is a deathly silence. Everyone is wide-eyed

Baron (*with difficulty*) Wasn't he the one who burnt down the *Comedie Française*?
Baroness Roasting an entire audience—?!
Isabel (*sipping her sherry*) Yeah—but the show stank!
Frau Lurker Und didn't he drop the chandelier at the *Paris Opera*?
Ygor Flattening the cheap seats?!
Isabel (*shrugging*) It got a laugh!
Baron (*askance*) It was *murder*!
Isabel (*with feeling*) Well, they shouldn't have booed me off-stage ... That was really *low*! Sure, folks said he over-reacted, but that's the artistic temperament for you. I mean, *I* was upset—but *he*, well, he was MAD! He *is* MAD!!

There is an insane laugh from The Phantom offstage

Baron But tell me, Miss Channing—why did those unwitting audiences boo you offstage?
Isabel (*glancing upwards nervously*) It was all *his* fault! He sent heavy letters to the managements telling them to give me a part—or else!
Baron (*producing his letter*) Letters like *this*?
Isabel Yeah. So many it was like confetti at a double weddin'! They couldn't refuse ... Nor could I—a girl's gotta eat! But, boy, was it a big mistake!
Baroness Why?
Isabel (*embarrassed*) I don't know if I dare tell you ...
Baron You *must*! It could be a matter of life or death!
Isabel For who?
All Us!!

Isabel OK—if you insist ...

Phantom (*off*) Sing for me, *ma cherie*! Sing for your Maestro! Sing! Sing!!

Isabel (*shouting*) That's the whole problem—I *can't*! So push off!! (*Turning to the others*) You know who I was billed as?

Baroness No.

Isabel Kiri Te Kanawa!!

Ygor What a bummer!

Isabel (*ruefully*) I should never have quit the Bluebell Girls!

Baron But why is the Phantom so keen that you sing, when you say you can't?

Isabel (*wryly*) He's a postive thinker!

Frau Lurker He's a *nut*!

Baron Ssh! He may hear us! Miss Channing—what do you expect me to do?

Isabel Either make me a prima donna ...

Baron Be realistic!

Isabel Or persuade the Masked Marauder to get off my back! Can you do that? How about hypnotism? Or a frontal lobotomy?

Baron Time-consuming and unpredictable. There is a much simper solution—

Isabel (*eagerly*) Yeah?

Baron Shoot to kill! Ygor—

Ygor Yes, Master?

Baron Find my revolver, load it and bring it back to me.

Ygor And if I meet the Phantom on the way?

Baron (*firmly*) Waste the bastard!

Ygor (*cheerfully*) Right on, Master!

Ygor exits DL

Baron I think your problem will be readily resolved, Miss Channing.

Isabel I sure hope so!

Baron And now, let us show you to your room.

Baron We have allotted you—(*wryly*)—the Maria Callas Suite!

Isabel Lead on!

The Baroness, the Baron and Isabel exit up the staircase

Isabel has left her suitcase behind. Frau Lurker goes to take the tray from the Monster

Frau Lurker These glasses need washing ... (*Sniffing*) Ja, und so do you!

The Monster moans

What was that?

The Monster moans again

Very well, if you have to ...

The Monster lumbers towards the door DL

But aim properly this time!

The Monster exits, followed by Frau Lurker

A second later the Phantom emerges from the wall R, *sniggering malevolently*

Phantom (*with passion*) The fools! They will never be able to outwit *me*! I 'ave more tricks up my sleeve than they possibly realize! (*He suddenly clutches at his sleeve and removes a stuffed mouse wich he throws away in disgust*) They will suffer the same 'ideous fate as those at the Opera when they mocked my beloved for 'itting a G flat instead of a top C! That she 'it a G flat was a feat in itself . . . But the fools would not appreciate it! Even when they were buried beneath an 'eap of cut glass! And, at the *Comedie*, when ma cherie sang Eurydice, they 'ad no notion 'ow much courage she displayed simply going on for the Concerto Duet—let alone facing its outcome! But I made them pay for their lack of appreciation! I made them see 'ow much faith I 'ad in 'er when they 'ad none! As the flames grew 'otter and their screams rose 'igher, *that* audience, at least, realized that there is more to Art than accuracy!! (*He laughs maniacally but breaks off as:*)

Isabel enters looking for her suitcase. She sees The Phantom and recoils

Isabel (*horrified*) It's *you*!!
Phantom (*smugly*) C'est moi!
Isabel Help!

Before she can flee The Phantom catches her in a tight embrace

Phantom (*grinning*) 'Allo, 'allo!
Isabel (*struggling*) Get your filthy murdering hands off of me!
Phantom Not until you 'ave 'eard what I 'ave to say, ma petite!
Isabel No way, José!
Phantom (*fiercely*) I took you from nowhere . . .
Isabel Are you kiddin'? I'd a solo spot at the *Moulin Rouge*!
Phantom Tried to make you sing . . .
Isabel What a hoot!
Phantom And this is 'ow you thank me—by 'iding with strangers!
Isabel (*frantically*) Let me go—freako!
Phantom They couldn't 'elp but 'ate me once they'd 'eard you speak!
Isabel What do you expect? They've got taste!
Phantom (*suddenly gentle*) Isabel . . . Cherie!
Isabel Don't you *dare* sweet talk me, you louse!
Phantom Say you'll be my love forever . . .
Isabel (*wide-eyed*) I knew it!
Phantom Say we'll live as one, together—
Isabel (*fervently*) I'm gonna *puke*!
Phantom Say the words and I will be your slave . . .
Isabel Get lost!!

She breaks free and brushes herself down, glaring at him

Phantom (*furious*) So—you want to reject me?!
Isabel You bet!
Phantom After all I 'ave done for you?
Isabel Mass murder an' makin' me look a lemon? Sure!!

The Phantom advances threateningly and she shrinks from him

Phantom (*pointing off*) Then *allez-vous*! Go!! (*Deadly*) But when you 'ear the midnight hour you will feel the Phantom's power! It will turn your blood to ice! I tell you now—it won't be nice!!

With a swirl of his cape the Phantom disappears back into the wall

Isabel hurriedly picks up her suitcase and heads for the staircase

Isabel (*as she goes*) Man, he sure is a lousy poet!

She bumps into Harry Talbot at the top of the stairs, but keeps on going

Talbot (*coming down the stairs*) Sorry, lady ... ! (*He moves C, looking uneasy. He suddenly scratches at his arms, then his chest, before glancing at his watch. Relieved*) You're all right yet, Harry boy! (*Frowning as he continues to scratch*) But I wish this damned itchin' wouldn't start up so soon. It's worse than *hives*! (*He goes to the window* UR, *pulls back the curtain and looks out warily. Singing*) "A room with a view, an' you— oooooo!" (*He growls in disgust and returns to* C) I hope to God the Baron comes up with the goods!

The Countess enters on the staircase, wearing evening dress and diamonds. She descends

Countess (*smiling*) Otherwise it will be another rough night?
Talbot (*dourly*) A *ruff*! night? You'd best believe it! (*Staring*) Have we met someplace—?
Countess (*moving to the sofa*) Here, five seconds ago ... I am the Countess Ilona Bathory.
Talbot Pleased to meet you.
Countess And I you, Mr Talbot.
Talbot You know me? How?
Countess Ygor pointed you out as we were coming downstairs.
Talbot (*warily*) What did he tell you?
Countess (*leisurely*) He said: "What do you call a man who sprouts fur, fangs and a tail? *Hairy Talbot*!"
Talbot (*dryly*) Ha-ha-ha.
Countess (*mischievously*) To which I replied: "He used to be a werewolf, but he's all right now-ooooo!"
Talbot That one's as old as the Ark!
Countess Well, Noah invented it! (*Staring at him*) So it's true, then—?
Talbot What?
Countess That you sprout fur, fangs—
Talbot An' a tail? You bet! It's an absolute riot—(*Scratching his backside*)—an' if I'm not quick on the striptease the last item plays merry hell with my chinos!

Countess You have my sympathy ...

Talbot (*wryly*) Great! It'll do wonders for me come midnight! (*He moves* DL)

Countess Don't go!

Talbot Why?

Countess (*rising*) I want to get to know you better.

Talbot (*with feeling*) Lady, you don't! I'm a pretty mean customer under the surface. Any dame I've dated will tell you that!

Countess But I find you fascinating ... You're not like any other man I've ever met.

Talbot That's 'cos I'm not like other men!

Countess Exactly. You're unaccountable—mysterious—and so ... so physical!

Talbot Yeah! Physically I can be a real dog!

Countess Frankly, Mr Talbot, I do not give a damn ... (*Moving towards him with a smile*) Come here—big boy ... !

Almost hypnotized, Talbot dance with the Countess to the tune of a saxophone playing "the blues" as:

The Count enters on the staircase and watches unseen. He gradually crosses from UL *to* UR

Talbot Aw hell—I don't need this ... Not now.

Countess Are you sure, Mr Talbot?

Talbot Positive!

Countess But why not?

Talbot (*desperately*) I gotta change!

Countess (*puzzled*) Into a wolf?

Talbot Naw—for dinner!

Talbot turns and races off up the staircase without seeing the Count, who moves forward once he has gone

Count (*drily*) So, Ilona—you have retained some of your motivation, I see.

Countess (*startled, then annoyed*) It is extremely rude to eavesdrop, Vlad!

Count (*bowing*) I apologize. But this castle has excellent acoustics. I could not help but overhear your—forgive me—not too subtle attempt to ensnare our furry friend.

Countess What are you insinuating? That I was being cheap?

Count A real bargain!

Countess That is outrageous! How dare you!

Count (*bowing*) Again, I apologize. (*Pointedly*) But when you have so ardently declared that your lifestye is unsatisfactory and that you are driven to distraction by casual encounters, how can I refrain from passing comment when I see you engaged in the very activity you profess to hate? It is a contradiction, and contradictions seldom escape notice or criticism.

Countess They seldom escape *your* notice! Why is it that wherever I go or whoever I meet you are somewhere in the vicinity? It is hardly coincidence!

Count No.

Countess Then what am I to assume? That you are spying on me! That, since I rejected you, you are determined to haunt my progress and spoil any happiness I may obtain!

Count (*shocked*) Ilona!

Countess It is true! Do not feign innocence. That "little boy" look would not fool a hamster! You have been following me consistently for the last twenty years!

The Count attempts to speak, but she will not let him

From California to Katmandu, from catacomb to crypt—wherever I am a bat you make your home! And your pathetic attempts at *disguise*! I may be dead, but I am certainly not blind! In New York, nineteen sixty-nine, you followed me as Caesar! In Weston-Super-Mare, nineteen seventy-five, you were Al Capone—and a month ago, in Cannes, not only were you stupid enough to wait at my table, you did so as Groucho Marx! I may be dissatisfied with reality, Vlad, but you are out of tune with it. You are totally ridiculous!

Count (*quietly*) It is because I love you, Ilona.

Countess Ha!

Count Do not mock me. I am sincere. Since our separation I am no longer logical—no longer rational.

Countess Were you ever?

Count Once, yes! My mental agility outstripped that of the Marquis de Sade! But now . . . (*Hesitantly*) Have you no sympathy?

Countess (*adamantly*) None! That evening in Cannes has left me colder than an Arctic Roll!

Count (*puzzled*) But it was a mild night.

Countess It was your jokes, Vlad, your abysmal jokes! I detest the Marx brothers . . . More to the point, I detest *you*!

Count You really mean that?

Countess Would you like it in writing? I could produce a thesis in five minutes!

Count (*heavily*) There is no need. I believe you.

Countess Good! Then perhaps you will be so considerate as to leave me alone until dinner when, unfortunately, we are obliged to meet again!

Count (*quietly*) As you wish.

Countess (*moving to the staircase*) And *please*—try to attend as you are now. Not some famous personality! I should like to enjoy my meal free from embarrassment—this time!

The Countess exits

He watches her leave and then moves D *frowning*

Count *Both* our fates lie with the Baron, Ilona. A man of ready promises it would seem . . . (*Musing*) To redeem your boredom and my torment he will have to be the world's greatest genius.

The Baron enters from DL, *carrying a pot plant which he is addressing sternly*

Baron So you'd try to *bite* me, would you? Well, see how you enjoy a night on the doorstep! (*Seeing the Count*) Oh, hello there! (*To the plant*) What was that? Don't be cheeky! You need to learn a few manners!

The Baron exits through the doors UR

Count (*looking confused*) But why do I have such grave doubts . . . ? After four hundred years am I finally becoming a pessimist? (*He shakes his head*) A few hours will tell—for soon it will be midnight! The time when my power and my appetite are at their strongest, when my restraint weakens and all mortals become my prey! (*Fiercely*) If you are a *fool*, Baron, and cannot cure my torment—then beware! Most of my *victims* have been *fools*!!

With a great swirl of his cloak he turns and strides towards the staircase as macabre music is heard and—

The CURTAIN *falls*

ACT II

SCENE 1

The same. Shortly before midnight

Before the CURTAIN *rises we hear the sound of very menacing music, which as the stage is revealed, quickly changes to 30s dance music. As the Lights come up we see Harry Talbot dancing with a very tipsy Isabel. The Baroness is sitting in the baronial chair, looking out of place. Ygor, now wearing a shabby tailcoat, is carrying round a tray of drinks. Frau Lurker has a dish of pretzels which she thrusts at people in a threatening fashion. The Countess is seated on the chair* R, *avoiding the glances of the Count, who is standing above her* UR. *The Monster stands behind the sofa, now acting as a standard lamp by wearing a large lampshade on his head and shining a torch beneath it. Everyone is now wearing evening dress*

As the music ends Isabel heads for the right side of the sofa and Talbot moves to sit to her left

Isabel (*excitedly*) Whoopee! I ain't had so much fun since Reagan did a prat-fall! You're a real nifty dancer, Harry!

Talbot Thanks.

Isabel Where d'you learn to move like that? Dance class?

Talbot No, I'm a natural.

Isabel You don't say?

Talbot (*drily*) I just *did*.

Baroness (*politely*) Do *you* dance, Count?

Count I do. But I am not enamoured of that particular style.

Talbot Too ambitious, huh?

Count (*sharply*) No—too *tame*! (*To the Countess*) Ilona–

Countess Vlad?

Count Let us demonstrate the *real* art of dance!

Countess (*reluctantly*) If we must ...

The Count and Countess move C

Talbot This had better be good!

Count (*turning to Talbot*) It will be!

Isabel Go to it, Drac!

To the strains of a powerful piece of classical music, the Count and Countess dance an extremely stylised pas de deux. *The others are stunned*

Count (*to Talbot at the dances conclusion*) Satisfied?

Talbot (*reluctantly*) Yeah ...

Isabel (*glancing round eagerly*) What's next

Frau Lurker (*pushing the dish at Isabel*) Another pretzel!

Isabel (*grimacing*) No, thanks. They taste like dog biscuits!

Frau Lurker So what? *Another!*

Isabel No!

Frau Lurker *Ja!* (*She throws one at her*) You must—you *will* be made welcome!

Isabel Honestly—this is the limit!

Frau Lurker (*fiercely*) There is *no* limit! *Eat!!*

Isabel (*nibbling it*) W-e-i-r-d!

Frau Lurker (*to Talbot*) Doggy biccy—*ja?*

Talbot (*glowering*) Swell.

Frau Lurker (*patting him on the head*) Good boy!

Talbot takes a pretzel, scowling

Countess (*suddenly*) Baroness—where is your husband?

Baroness In the laboratory, I think ... But there's a rather chatty Tradescantia in the annexe, so he may have been held back.

Talbot (*with feeling*) I hope to God he hasn't—it's nearly *midnight!* I can't hang around much longer! (*He scratches at his arms and shoulders*)

Baroness (*puzzled*) Why not?

Ygor (*grinning*) Things may get rather *hairy*, mistress!

Talbot Smart alec! (*Reaching down, he starts loosening his shoes*)

Count I, too, am getting rather impatient. The night is calling and I must *obey!*

Isabel *I* can't hear anything.

Count That is because mortal ears are unable to detect the subtle sounds of darkness!

Isabel Oh, we *are* superior, aren't we!

Count *We* are. You are only a *pleb!*

Isabel (*rising*) Want to bet? See here, buster—!

Countess (*sharply*) This is no time for arguments! We must be *calm!*

Isabel sits reluctantly

Ygor Shame. I love a scrap!

Count (*to the Countess*) *Calm?* How can you expect me to be calm, knowing as you *do*, the voracious appetite which overtakes our kind at the final stroke of the midnight bell?!

Ygor (*excitedly*) The bell! The bell!

All Shut up!

Countess (*to the Count*) You could *subdue* it.

Count (*agonized*) I cannot!

Countess That is because you're a greedy pig!

Count (*appalled*) Countess!

Frau Lurker (*advancing on the Count*) Have a pretzel!

Count (*snarling*) I do not want a pretzel! (*Thunderously*) I want *blood!!*

Everyone is stunned

Isabel (*sotto voce*) Oh—*gross!*

Baroness (*delicately*) Well, I'm afraid we can't help you *there*.

Count (*eyeing her sinisterly*) Oh yes, you can, Baroness. Indeed you *can* . . . !

The Count moves towards the Baroness. Everyone is transfixed

Countess (*alarmed*) Vlad—*no!*

The Count is reaching for the Baroness's throat when:

The Baron enters jauntily from DL *carrying a flask full of fluid*

Baron Success! Triumph! (*Seeing everyone's faces*) Hello, what's going on?

Count (*gutturally*) Nothing . . .

The Count backs away from the Baroness, who has a hand at her throat. The Baron is oblivious to the tension. He moves C *as the Baroness returns to her seat*

Baron (*proudly*) Ladies and gentlemen, after much careful thought and some frantic rooting around for the right ingredients, I have, I believe, distilled the solution to *all* your problems!

Talbot (*loosening his shoes even more*) About time, too!

Baron (*holding up the flask*) The antidote is a combination of Wolfsbane flowers and cloves of garlic . . .

Isabel grimaces. The Baron sniffs the air

Someone's feet are a bit niffy!

Frau Lurker (*pointing to Talbot*) *His!*

Count (*impatiently*) Get on with it!

Baron Well, as I was saying, this mixture, once consumed—

Isabel (*to Talbot*) Rather you than me!

Talbot snarls and Isabel recoils

Baron (*glaring at them*) Will rid you of all your unsociable symptoms, leaving you free to live the normal life you are so earnestly seeking!

There is polite applause from the members of the household. The Baron nods in appreciation

(*Wryly*) Of course, you may have to suck *mints* for a day or two—

Talbot (*growling*) Just give us the *dose!*

Baron Very well. Ygor—!

Ygor (*hurrying forward*) Yes, Master?

Baron (*handing him the flask*) Pour a glass for each of our guests . . .

Ygor ambles round the Hall doing so

Isabel (*wide-eyed*) Not *me*, surely?

Baron Not necessarily. (*Musing*) Although it might do something to enhance your charm!

Isabel (*bridling*) Well, that's nice! Thanks a bunch!

The guests' glasses, apart from Isabel's, have now been filled. The Baron has been given a glass of sherry by the Baroness

Baron (*raising his glass*) My friends—I give you a toast ... Happiness and Normality!
All Happiness and Normality!

They drink, most of them grimacing, and then The Phantom's voice is heard

Phantom (*off*) Did I not warn you what would 'appen if you interfered with my plans? Be'old your potion, Baron! It is not the antidote you think!

There is a simultaneous reaction from the others

Count What does he mean?
Countess Who is that?
Talbot What's going on?
The Others It's the *Phantom*!

The Baron rushes to Ygor and grabs the flask from him. He sniffs and tastes it—then looks horrified

Phantom (*off*) You fool! You did not listen! So be it! The witching hour is upon you—and the calamity I foretold will now occur!!

There is a second's silence and the castle clock begins to strike midnight

Ygor (*wildly*) The clock! The clock! (*He mechanically counts the strokes*)
Countess (*aghast*) It's *midnight*!
Count (*clutching his throat*) What is *happening*?

Talbot begins to contort, bending forwards and scratching his backside furiously

Isabel (*watching Talbot*) I dunno—but it sure is *kinky*!
Talbot (*agonized*) The *change*—it's *starting*!!
Countess (*a hand to her brow*) I feel *strange*! Baron, your potion—!
Baron (*desperately*) Not mine! His! The *Phantom*'s!
Countess It's making me *ill*!
Count (*malevolently*) It's making me *ravenous*!
Baroness (*hiding behind the Baron*) Oh no!

Talbot suddenly tears off his shoes to reveal fur-covered feet

Talbot (*snarling*) I gotta get outta here!
Count (*fiercely*) That makes two of us!
Talbot (*tearing at his clothes*) I gotta get outta here *now-oooooo*! (*As he howls he doubles up so that his chest is thrust between his knees*)
Baroness (*weakly*) Feel free.

Talbot springs from the sofa to land on all fours. A wolf's tail protrudes from the seat of his trousers

Isabel (*pointing*) Oo-er!
Talbot (*feeling behind him*) Damn! That's *another* pair-rrrrr!

Growling and snarling Talbot moves behind the sofa, stalking Ygor, who quickly retreats

Ygor (*wildly*) Sanctuary! Sanctuary!
Countess (*heading for the staircase*) I want the bathroom!
Count (*ferociously*) You want *blood!*
Countess No—the bathroom! I'm going to throw up!

The Countess exits hurriedly

Baroness (*calling after her*) Second on the left—mind the step!
Frau Lurker (*advancing on the Count*) A pretzel!
Count (*pushing her aside*) Out of my way—hag!

The Count storms out UR

Sinister organ music begins loudly

Baron What on earth?!
Baroness The Phantom!
Isabel (*rising*) I knew it! He's doing his Dr Phibes routine! Honest to God— it's so hackneyed!

Isabel turns and sees Talbot stalking her. His hands are now as furry as his feet, and when he snarls he reveals sharp teeth

(*Alarmed*) Get away from me, you creep! Help!

Talbot starts chasing Isabel round the Hall, in the course of which she bumps into the Monster, whose light goes out. Moaning loudly he, too, starts blundering round the Hall, still wearing the lampshade. Frau Lurker throws pretzels in an attempt to distract Talbot from pursuing Isabel

Ygor (*to Talbot*) Sit! *Down* boy!
Frau Lurker There's a nice doggy! Walkies!!
Baroness (*to the Baron over the confusion*) Victor, what did he give them? It wasn't *poison*?
Baron (*grimly*) Very nearly! A mixture of cod liver and castor oils! (*Shouting upwards and brandishing a fist*) Phantom—I don't know how you managed it, but I'm going to get you for this! D'you hear? You'd better stay *hidden*—because if you *don't*, my meddlesome freak, the next calamity will be *yours*!!

The Baroness attempts to calm the Baron as The Phantom's maniacal laughter rings out over the organ music and the onstage chaos as—

The Lights fade to black-out

Scene 2

Immediately following

When the Lights come up the stage is empty. Eerie up-tempo music begins and Isabel dances on to stage from the staircase. After a moment, the doors up R open and the Count enters unseen by Isabel. He approaches her stealthily, arms outstretched. At the last minute she turns and sees him ...

The following sequences occur simultaneously:

A) The Count chases Isabel off up the staircase.
   The Baron, the Baroness, Ygor and Frau Lurker rush out of the door DL, across the stage and out of the doors UR.
   The Phantom sneaks out of the secret panel and rushes out DL.

B) The Monster chases the Phantom from off DL, across the stage and out of the doors UR.
   Talbot chases the Baron, the Baroness, Ygor and Frau Lurker from off UR, across the stage and off up the staircase.
   The Count chases the Countess from off UL down the staircase and out of the door DL.
   Isabel rushes down the staircase, across the stage and out of the doors UR.

C) The Phantom chases Isabel from off UR across the stage. She disappears off up the staircase. He rushes back to the panel and vanishes behind it.
   The Baron, the Baroness, Ygor and Frau Lurker rush down the staircase and out of the door DL.
   The Count chases the Countess out of the door DL. He crosses to the doors UR and exits. She rushes off up the staircase.

After a moment, the Baroness emerges from the door DL onto the now empty stage and creeps around, reacting with fright to the music and imagined sounds. The Count enters through the doors UR and approaches her unseen, arms outstretched. At the last minute she turns and sees him ...

Again, the following sequences occur simultaneously:

A) The Count chases the Baroness off DL.
   Talbot chases Isabel down the staircase, across the stage and out of the doors UR.
   The Phantom emerges from the panel; the Baron, armed with a revolver, emerges from the door DL. They see each other and the Baron chases the Phantom off up the staircase.

B) Ygor, brandishing a cross, and Frau Lurker, hurling garlic cloves, chase the Count from off DL, across the stage and out of the doors UR.
   The Countess chases the Baron down the staircase and off DL.
   The Monster chases Isabel through the doors UR, across the stage and off up the staircase.

C) Talbot chases Ygor and Frau Lurker through the doors UR. They rush off DL. He races off up the staircase.

The Baroness, armed with a meat cleaver, chases the Countess through the door DL, across the stage and off up the staircase.

Isabel, chased by the Phantom, who is chased by the Monster, rushes down the staircase. She and the Monster exit through the doors UR

The Baron, still armed with the revolver, emerges from the door DL, sees the Phantom and chases him to the panel. The Phantom disappears, leaving the Baron pounding on the wall. He then turns to see the Monster, carrying a prostrate Isabel in his arms, enter UR, cross the stage and disappear off up the staircase. The Baron shrugs and then exits hurriedly through the door L as the music ends and—

The Lights fade to black-out

SCENE 3

One o'clock in the morning

When the Lights come up the stage is empty. A wolf howl is heard, followed by a scream, and then Isabel rushes down into the Hall from the staircase, breathless

Isabel (*fervently*) Monsters, monsters everywhere—and not a drop to drink! It's enough to drive one bug-house! (*She moves* C) There's enough fur an' fangs round here to start a zoo! But one thing's for sure—*this* girl's not goin' to wind up as someone's midnight snack! (*She sees the sherry decanter*) Saved by jingo! There's still a drop of the old Amontillado!

As she goes to pour herself a glass, The Phantom emerges from the wall R, *stealthily*

(*Singing badly*) "I'd love to meet a matador—é Viva Espana!"
Phantom (*softly*) Sing for me! Sing, ma cherie!
Isabel (*turning*) What?! Oh no, not *you* again!
Phantom Oui, c'est moi! Why? Did you think I 'ad gone for good?
Isabel Give me credit! You're harder to shake off than a Book Club! (*Sipping sherry*) But I never expected you back so *soon*. What happened? Did your organ blow up?!
Phantom Non.
Isabel That's something! All those Toccatas and Fugues—it's a wonder it isn't knackered!
Phantom Pas du tout. It is very robust for its age.
Isabel Quit boasting! Why are you here?
Phantom I find you irresistible!
Isabel You *must* if you've managed to dodge the gang of freaks roamin' around out there! How did you do it?
Phantom (*wryly*) Using all my skill in deception, of course.
Isabel You mean you ran like hell!

Phantom Oui. (*Moving towards her*) The risks were enormous, but I 'ad to take them. 'Ow else could I catch a glimpse of you?
Isabel (*drily*) So why are we face to face?
Phantom I am shortsighted.
Isabel You sure are! Have you any idea what you *did* tonight? You didn't just miff the Baron, but all those poor folks who came here for his help!
Phantom Those "poor folks" are monsters, ma cherie!
Isabel Well, you're no Peter Perfect! Think of all the rotten things you've done!
Phantom They were all for you, ma petite—!
Isabel "Say it with funerals"—was that the idea? (*Forcibly*) Come off it— you ran riot simply because it gave you a cheap thrill!

The Phantom shrugs

An' you'd have done the same tonight if there'd been a chandelier or a box of matches handy!
Phantom Peut-être.
Isabel See! You're nothing but a devious, egocentric, obsessive, tyrannical pyromaniac! An' you give me the *creeps*!
Phantom You are honest, at least.
Isabel Yep!
Phantom So there is no 'ope for us at all?
Isabel Bullseye, buster!
Phantom But why? Tell me why?
Isabel (*raising her eyes*) Boy, are some guys gluttons for punishment! (*With forced patience*) Listen, charmless, not only are a lot of your little habits a real turn-off, but when it comes to physical appeal you're distinctly minus. You know what I'm saying? Especially in the facial department. That I think one can politely describe as zero!
Phantom But you 'ave never seen my face!
Isabel Mister—that's the whole point!
Phantom (*fiercely*) Nor do you want to! The unkind star which 'as made me a social nuisance 'as also prevented me from 'aving friends by giving me this face— this mockery of 'umanity—which terrifies all 'oo see it! Even my own mother disowned me! Can you imagine the shame I 'ave endured ever since that 'ideous day when I discovered that I'd been dumped, 'elpless, on an 'ill outside Rouen, to be raised by a family of 'edge 'ogs!
Isabel They can't have been very choosy!
Phantom They weren't! But then 'edge 'ogs know very little about European 'istory, political leaders or World War Two.
Isabel What are you getting at?
Phantom Turn and see. Could anything other than an 'edge 'og endure a face such as this?! (*He removes his mask to reveal a face which is the spitting image of Hitler*)

Isabel gasps and recoils

Now you know the full extent of my secret, what 'ave you to say?
Isabel (*adamant*) The same as I've said all along—gross, no way and Auf Wiedersehen, pet! I'm off! (*She heads for the staircase*)

Phantom (*pleading*) But Isabel—!
Isabel (*as she goes*) Adieu, *Adolf*!

Isabel exits up the stairs

Phantom (*gazing up after her, sadly*) You will never be my love for ever . . .
We will never live as one, together . . .

Another wolf howl is heard, followed by a scream and a yell

Ygor and Frau Lurker rush in from DL

The Phantom freezes

Frau Lurker (*saluting*) Heil Hitler!
Phantom (*disgusted*) Ach!

The Phantom turns and disappears into the wall R

Ygor gapes after him

Ygor (*to Frau Lurker*) Was that—?
Frau Lurker (*nodding*) Of course!
Ygor But I thought he was dead and living in Brazil—?
Frau Lurker Rot! He has been the landlord of a Bierkellar in Prague for the
last twelve years!
Ygor How do you know?
Frau Lurker I worked there! It is called "*The Happy Jew*" . . . (*Proudly*)
Und we were on first name terms!
Ygor (*awed*) You called him Adolf?
Frau Lurker Nein—Hans.
Ygor (*musing*) I wondered . . .
Frau Lurker (*gesticulating quickly*) So did *his*!
Ygor If you ever called him—(*whispering*)—*you* know—Der Führer—?
Frau Lurker Only on pay day!
Ygor Oh! What's *your* first name?
Frau Lurker Brunnhilde!
Ygor Snappy.
Frau Lurker Und what is yours, Ygor?
Ygor (*nonplussed*) Ygor.
Frau Lurker I was just checking. No-one is quite what they seem.
Ygor (*ruefully*) Especially that crowd out there! Talk about two-faced!
Two-fanged's more like it!
Frau Lurker Ja—und they give me the shivers!
Ygor (*grimly*) They give me the hump!
Frau Lurker (*mystified*) What—*another*?
Ygor Don't be daft! One's enough!
Frau Lurker *Ja!* Two und you'd look even more like a camel!
Ygor (*wryly*) Thanks!

Suddenly a wolf howls and the door DL *begins to open. They cling to each
other, terrified. It is only the Baron however*

He enters nervously, then relaxes when he sees the others

Baron Oh, it's only you . . .

Frau Lurker *Ja*—only us!

Ygor No hairy, toothy types in *here*, Master!

Frau Lurker (*dourly*) Not yet!

Baron (*nervously*) Have you seen any of them?

Ygor The Count is up on the chimney.

Baron Good!

Frau Lurker The Countess is in the garden.

Baron Excellent!

Ygor And Mr Talbot's in the larder.

Baron What's he doing there?

Frau Lurker Gnawing a bone. He was peckish.

Baron (*warily*) And The Phantom—?

Both (*exchanging glances*) We don't know.

Baron Damn! He's the biggest troublemaker of the lot.

Ygor (*suddenly*) He might be with *Hitler*, Master.

Baron (*askance*) What?

Frau Lurker (*quickly*) Nonsense! Hitler is dead!

Ygor (*wide-eyed*) But—?

Baron (*irritably*) Of course he is! Now clear off, both of you. But if you see
any of the guests heading this way distract them. Chat, play cards,
anything—but I've got to have time to make up another antidote!

Ygor Anything you say, Master . . .

Ygor and Frau Lurker move DL

So *we're* the ones who have to risk our necks! I like that!

Frau Lurker (*sternly*) It is all in the line of duty. Shut up!

Ygor (*opening the door*) You would have been great in the S.S.!

Frau Lurker (*proudly*) I *was*!

They both exit

*The Baron paces up and down, frowning. He looks at his watch, grimaces and
then moves forward*

Baron (*urgently*) What the hell am I going to do? Come dawn and they'll all
cool off, but that's hours away . . . Anything could happen between now
and then! I could be bitten, mauled, clawed, seduced or deafened by organ
music—and none of it appeals! (*Musing*) Well, perhaps I don't mind being
seduced, but as for the *rest*—! (*With feeling*) I'm young—I've got the best
part of life in front of me! I don't want to die at the hands—or paws—of a
group of blood-crazed loonies! It isn't fair!! (*Suddenly*) I'll speak to
Elisabeth! She'll know what to do—!

As he turns towards the staircase another wolf howl is heard, then a scream

The Baroness races downstairs with a suitcase

Baroness Victor, I'm leaving!

Baron Oh, fine! Just when I need all the help I can get!

Baroness You've never needed *my* help and I doubt if you ever will. So
don't try to make me feel a heel—it won't work!

Baron And just where do you plan on going?

Baroness The village, to start with. There's a very cosy inn, moderately priced, which—unlike *this* mortuary—has beds one can sleep in! Then, tomorrow, when the fog has lifted and you've died a horrible death, I shall travel to Mother's via Budapest.

Baron I envy you!

Baroness Sarcasm doesn't become you, Victor. Best leave it to me ... I shall send you a postcard, of course—assuming that there's no need for a wreath, which I'm not.

Baron (*drily*) Thanks!

Baroness It's the least I can do—although much depends on whether I have easy access to a post-office or a florist's. But I shall do my best.

Baron What, may I ask, has produced this sudden urge to fly-by-night?

Baroness If that was a pun, Victor, it was exceedingly feeble and should only be applied to those of your guests with that tendency. *I* am normal, and like any normal person have a great aversion to creatures which threaten my existence. (*Passionately*) And this place is swarming with them!

Baron So *that's* why you're leaving.

Baroness Yes, Victor, that is why. After a short period of deliberation—the time it took for Mr Talbot to drop on all fours and the Count to reveal his canines—I decided that living here really *isn't* my scene. I am now cherishing the small, but very attractive hope that out there I may encounter people—dare I say it—like me. Neither scientific, sinister nor sub-normal—but nice people. Human beings, in fact! Do you take my point?

Baron Yes Elisabeth. But you won't find them easy to come by.

Baroness Why not?

Baron Nice people went out with the Dodo!

Baroness (*heading for the doors* UR) So did your common sense. Goodbye, Victor!

Baron (*pleading*) Elisabeth!

Baroness (*opening the door*) May you rest in peace!

The Baroness exits, slamming the door behind her

Baron (*angrily*) Damn!

A wolf howl is heard close by and the Baron's expression changes to one of fear

Oh hell ... !

He hurries out of the door DL

A second later Harry Talbot appears at the head of the staircase and starts slinking down it. He is now stripped to the waist, totally hairy, with wolfish features

Talbot (*as he reaches* C; *growling*) I should have known this would happen! Every time a guy says he'll help me it winds up bein' a total wash-out! An' it's me who looks the jerk—no-one else! Which of them's got fur, paws an' a snout to beat Barry Manilow's? You tell *me*! An' as for dressin' for dinner—well, white tie an' tails takes on a completely new meanin'! An' how—oooooooo!

The Phantom emerges from the wall R

Talbot snarls and The Phantom freezes

(*Growling*) Who the hell are you?

Phantom (*awkwardly*) I don't really know. They call me The Phantom of the Opera.

Talbot (*realizing*) Then it was *you* who cocked-up my antidote!

Phantom I'm afraid so.

Talbot (*savagely*) I'm gonna *kill* you, you punk!

Phantom (*recoiling*) Non! Don't!

Talbot (*snarling*) Why not?

Phantom (*urgently*) Because I didn't realize what I was doing—'oo you were—what your problems are—!

Talbot Bull!

Phantom It's true! I 'ad no idea until I saw what 'appened to you all at midnight! I was only trying to embarrass the Baron.

Talbot You sure embarrassed *me*! Look at me! How would you fancy windin' up like this—hey?

Phantom I wouldn't! I'm sorry.

Talbot (*growling*) Sure!

Phantom I mean it! I can associate with such affliction.

Talbot Come off it! There's no brush sticking' outta your pants!

Phantom *Non.* But then you don't 'ave a face like this!

He removes his mask and Talbot recoils with a yelp

Talbot Cripes! I thought you were dead!

Phantom (*petulantly*) I am not 'itler!

Talbot You could have fooled me!

Phantom I was born like this!

Talbot What? With the 'tache?

Phantom (*bitterly*) With the 'tache.

Talbot You poor devil!

Phantom Pity accomplishes nothing, Monsieur Talbot ... (*Eagerly*) But it is welcome nonetheless! I get very little else.

Talbot (*wryly*) I'm not surprised!

Phantom (*sadly*) We are very similar, you and I. We are both alone in the world, frustrated by our condition and unable to find any succour to 'elp us through.

Talbot If I could find a sucker I'd load all this onto him! I sure don't want it!

Phantom Nor I this face! But it seems we 'ave no choice in the matter. Like the 'unchback, we just 'ave to—

Talbot Lump it?

Phantom Oui.

Talbot (*growling*) But I don't want to lump it! I've had enough of bein' the four-legged friend! I want to be an ordinary guy like I was before—still good-lookin', mind—but ordinary ... Not Wolfman Jack!

Phantom But 'ow can you achieve that?

Talbot (*miserably*) Hell, I dunno. Any suggestions?

Phantom We could wait. The Baron may yet provide 'ope.

Talbot Are you sure?

Phantom Monsieur—I am an eternal optimist.

Talbot With a mug like that I guess you'd have to be! I say, fella—

Phantom What?

Talbot Will you do me a big favour an' take me outside?

Phantom You'd like a breath of fresh air? Bien sûr!

The Phantom and Talbot move UR

Talbot That, an' maybe chase a stick or two. I'm feelin' frisky!

Phantom (*opening the door*) So long as you're a good boy and bring them back!

Talbot Sure! Lead on, McAdolf!

Phantom (*drily*) Ha-ha-ha!

The Phantom and Talbot exit

The Lights fade to Black-out

SCENE 4

A few minutes later

When the Lights come up the stage is deserted. The sound of bats calling and flying suddenly fills the air. A second later the Countess descends, the staircase lowering her arms. Her face is wary. As she reaches C *the Count sweeps in* UR, *also lowering his arms and looking furious*

Count Why do you persist in avoiding me?

Countess I am not avoiding you. You exaggerate terribly, Vlad.

Count Is it an exaggeration to say you slid forty feet down that outside drainpipe when I stepped on the roof?

Countess No ...

Count Or that you did a hundred yards sprint from the terrace to the stables when I appeared at the back door?

Countess That is also true.

Count Then since I was the common denominator in both of these athletic stunts, I assume you must have been avoiding me!

Countess If you insist.

Count Ilona, you infuriate me with your affected calm! It is not natural!

Countess But what *is* natural where we are concerned? Answer me that.

Count This quibbling, too, is beyond my understanding. We have known each other for centuries. You know all the rules!

Countess (*sharply*) I do! And I fail to see what is suddenly so wrong about
sliding down drainpipes and sprinting long distances when I have been
doing such things for centuries!

Count Ha!

Countess Who is it who invents the "rules" anyway? Could it be you?

Count Yes, it is I. I, Count Dracula, the king of vampires! I have laid down
the rules of conduct, and the most important of these is that you do not go
against your nature if you are, as we are, members of the Undead. And
this, Ilona, you are doing! You are going against your nature and that is.
why you are avoiding me—because you are fearful of criticism. Most
justified criticism!

Countess (*applauding*) Bravo! Bravo! You have finally answered your own
question!

Count (*with narrowed eyes*) Are you mocking me? Because if you are—

Countess Do I detect a threat? I think I do. But please, continue.

Count You will not make me angry. I will not give you the satisfaction! But
hear this: you are alienating yourself from your own kind through this
perverse pursuit of a new lifestyle. You cannot hope to find happiness.

Countess Why not?

Count I know from bitter experience!

Countess Bitter? When you have revelled in every unsociable act our kind
are capable of performing! Who do you think you are fooling? Every
night for centuries you have been as happy as a sandboy—tormenting
helpless mortals for pleasure as much as need!

Count (*sharply*) You accuse *me* of self-indulgence? What about you? All
those innocents—men *and* women—you used to lure to your castle! And
for what? It was no whist drive!

Countess No ...

Count Your activities were more notorious than Lucrezia Borgia's!

Countess The world was different then.

Count Yes—thanks to you it was depopulated!

Countess At least *I* learned to moderate my appetite!

Count (*drily*) You didn't learn—you had to!

Countess What do you mean?

Count Innocence is a thing of the past!

Countess (*ruefully*) True. But that is not the only reason. There has to be
more to life than moonlight, malevolence and misery—and I am determined to seek it out!

Count What you ask is impossible! We are as we are—vampires, creatures
who prey on the blood of the living and who cannot do as they do, despite
our deepest, most secret longings. To survive we must stay true to our
identity. (*Forcibly*) We are children of the night—and we can never
change!

Countess Are you so certain?

Count Yes, I can hardly have survived for so long without that certainty!

Countess (*drily*) You have survived, Vlad, simply because you are a mean
bastard, and that is all! You cannot change because you don't want to. I
do and I will!

Count (*viciously*) So you still believe the Baron will be your saviour?

Countess Yes, and nothing you say will deter me from holding onto that hope.

Count And to hold onto you, Ilona, what am I expected to do?

Countess Nothing. I refuse to give you any advice. You are more obdurate than the walls of this castle. If you cannot see the path to the goal I'm seeking, I cannot hope to make your way clear. You must accept this— and lose me!

Count (*angrily*) Ach! We shall see!

Countess Indeed we shall.

There is a distant roll of thunder

> *The Baron creeps in, looking behind him. It is only once he has closed the door that he turns and sees the others*

Baron (*awkwardly*) Oh—hello.

Countess Good morning, Baron.

Baron Morning? Yes—I suppose it is.

Count (*pointedly*) Have you distilled another antidote for us? Or is it to be as the first was—a no-no?

Baron Yes—I mean, no!

Countess What do you mean?

Baron I need more time!

There is a flash of lightning and the Baron jumps

Count Why?

Baron I—I've run out of ingredients!

Countess Are you saying that you have no immediate solution?

Baron (*wryly*) Not even a Disprin! (*Sotto voce*) And boy, do I need one!

Count (*menacing*) That is not good enough, my friend. Not good at all!

There is another roll of thunder, closer this time

> *The doors UR open to admit The Phantom and Talbot*

The Baron freezes at the sight of them

Talbot (*advancing*) Just the guy we were looking for!

Phantom Indeed.

Baron (*to the Phantom; drily*) Phantom, I had hoped you would appear. This is truly a delight! For now we're finally mask to face, you've really made my night!

There is another flash of lightning. The Baron suddenly produces a gun which he levels at The Phantom's chest

Phantom (*calmly*) Monsieur—rhyming couplets are no way to greet a guest.

Baron (*deadly*) You aren't my guest! You're a miserable gate-crasher and you've botched up all my plans! First you threaten me, then you dislodge half a ton of plaster knocking about in the damp course, and finally, to top it all, you go and spike my antidote and bust four keys on the Wurlitzer! Phantom—you're dead!!

The Baron fires the gun to the accompaniment of another roll of thunder. The Phantom staggers but is surprised to find he is unharmed

Phantom (*nonplussed*) I must be! Nothing 'urts.

Baron (*checking the gun*) Damn! That blockhead Ygor's given me blanks!

Count You are a lucky man, Phantom.

Phantom I would not go so far as to say that—but it was a close shave, which we can all do without.

Talbot (*growling*) Speak for yourself!

Countess Baron, you are a great disappointment to me. I had hoped you would devote yourself to research on our behalf—not our destruction!

Baron He deserves it! Don't you realize he's the one who prevented you from achieving normality? Just when we were on the brink of success!

There is another flash of lightning

Phantom (*drily*) Were we, Baron?

Baron (*warily*) What do you mean?

Phantom The antidote you 'ad prepared . . . Are you so sure it would 'ave worked?

Baron Of course! Do you doubt my scientific genius?

Phantom Pas du tout. Merely the purgative effect of Bovril—for that was the nature of your antidote!

The Baron looks ashamed, the others furious

Count Is that true, Herr Baron?

Baron I'm afraid so.

Countess But why?

Talbot (*snarling*) Because he's a con-man, that's why!

Count And a very definite failure!

Thunder rolls again

Baron (*desperately*) All right, all right—I admit it. I am a failure! But it's not through want of trying! I tell you, I could do wonders here—things which would astound scientific minds the world over . . . And why can't I? Because I made the mistake of building a laboratory in the back of beyond! Where there's no electricity, no intelligent man power—God, there isn't even a Boots to provide me with supplies! D'you blame me for pretending when the only medical kit I get comes from local cemeteries! It's no wonder my wife's left me . . . She knows she married a screwball!!

There is a vivid flash of lightning

Count (*fiercely*) Confession comes too late. You must pay the price for this deception!

Countess (*icily*) We placed all our hopes in you—and you have betrayed us!

Baron (*desperately*) Have you no pity?

Talbot (*menacingly*) It's too late for pity, fella!

Baron I've told you the truth! Show some compassion!

Phantom (*deadly*) The world showed no compassion to us!

Baron But why make me pay for the sins of others? *I* didn't make you the way you are! Friends—be fair!

Count We will. You will die reasonably quickly!

Baron (*recoiling*) Stay away from me!

There is another crash of thunder

> *Ygor and Frau Lurker enter* DL. *Isabel enters from the staircase*

Ygor (*wildly*) Master! Master! The monsters, they're heading—(*seeing them*)—this ... way ...

Baron (*acidly*) Ygor— you're inept!

Ygor (*pleased*) Am I? Thank you, Master!

Frau Lurker What is happening?

Isabel Are you playin' party games?

Count We are about to rip the Baron limb from limb!

Isabel That's a new one ...

Lightning flashes again

Ygor But Master—we haven't been paid!

Baron Tough! (*Turning to the others*) As for you—you're all mad, d'you hear? MAD!!

Talbot (*growling*) Yeah—mad for your blood, mister! (*To the others*) So let's go get it!!

They begin to seize the Baron

Baron NO!!

There is the most terrific roll of thunder yet, and as it occurs the door DL *opens*

> *The Baroness enters*

Baroness (*sharply*) Stop this—at once!

Everyone freezes

Baron (*happily*) Elisabeth! You've come back!

Baroness (*simply*) I never left, Victor.

Baron (*pointing* UR; *puzzled*) But you went out of those doors—?

Baroness And came in the back way! I could hardly leave you at the mercy of these ... people.

Ygor What mercy?

Baroness Exactly. (*To the others*) Let him go!

Count Baroness, I admire your loyalty, but you should not be interfering in this matter. Your husband has misled and betrayed us!

Baroness (*firmly*) Misled, certainly—but not betrayed you. His crime has simply been wishful thinking. He wanted to help you—led you all to believe he could—but when it came to the crunch he lacked the means to do so. That was unfortunate—

Talbot I'll say!

Baroness But in the end he was brave enough to admit his mistake. Doesn't that mean something? Doesn't it prove that we are all, irrespective of individual tendencies, fallible? He no less than you! My friends, in sailing the seas of this unpredictable life we are all in the same boat!

Ygor Yes—the *Titanic*.

Baroness Shut up! You cannot blame him for being as unlucky as you are—! Spare him . . .

There is the sound of fading thunder and then the Baron is released from their clutches

Baron (*wiping his brow*) Phew!

Countess (*dismally*) So, after all our hopes, there is to be no solution, no end to this nightmare of ours?

Baroness Did I say that?

Phantom Non, mais—

Baroness Wait a moment. (*She rings the bell*)

Ygor The bells! The—(*seeing their faces*) Forget it!

The door DL opens and the Monster enters carrying a tray containing eight glasses of liquid

Baroness (*gesturing*) Here is your antidote! Take a glass, each of you.

All Each of us?

Baroness (*smiling*) Yes. After tonight you can *all* do with a tonic, I'm sure.

Isabel (*as she takes a glass*) It doesn't look like tonic to me!

Baroness Believe me, it will do you the power of good. *I* should know—we've already tried it!

Baron (*puzzled*) We have?

Monster (*calmly; well spoken*) Yes, sir.

Baron What the—?!

Monster You will find it a total success, sir. It has exceptional qualities and no side effects whatsoever.

The Baron is speechless

Baroness (*taking his arm; affectionately*) Science has to have its guinea pigs, Victor—and we were the only ones available.

Talbot (*peering into his glass; suspiciously*) This tastes like lager!

Phantom Mais oui!

Baroness That's because it is lager . . The kind which refreshes the parts which other beers cannot reach! Drink it. You won't be sorry.

Warily they do so—and gradually their faces lighten

Baron I feel *different*. (*To the Baroness; appreciatively*) Elisabeth—!

Baroness (*affectionately*) Darling . . .

Baron You look wonderful!

Baroness (*nodding*) I know.

Count (*suddenly*) I don't feel *hungry* anymore.

Countess (*wide-eyed*) I don't feel *miserable*.

Isabel I want to *sing*!

Frau Lurker I want to *smile*!

Phantom I want to be *Richard Clayderman*!
Ygor I want to be *Richard the Third*!
All It's worked! The stuff's *worked*!
Monster (*calmly*) I told you it would. (*Raising his eyes*) Oh, ye of little
    faith—!

Talbot is the only one who hasn't reacted and now he gasps and clutches his
stomach

All What's wrong?
Talbot I feel *bad*!
Count What? (*Turning*) Baroness—?
Talbot Don't worry—it's not the beer. It's all that marrowbone I ate earlier.
    It must have disagreed with—! (*Wide-eyed*) 'Scuse me, folks!!

Talbot claps a hand to his mouth and races off up the staircase

The others relax

Count (*extending a hand to the Countess*) Ilona . . .
Countess (*taking it*) Vlad . . .
Isabel (*extending a hand to The Phantom*) Lover boy . . .
Phantom (*taking it*) Ma petite!
Frau Lurker (*extending a hand to Ygor*) Coochie!
Ygor (*taking it*) Diddums!
Monster (*askance*) Who wrote this—?!
Baron Elisabeth—?
Baroness Yes, darling?
Baron How did you know I'd admitted to my mistakes? You weren't here.
Baroness Not here exactly, but close enough. (*Pointing* DL) I was on the
    other side of that door! (*Smiling*) It was very noble of you, Victor.
Baron (*straightening up*) Not at all. I was simply being honest. What's life
    worth without honesty or honour or—
Baroness Love?
Baron (*grinning*) Yes, damn it! (*Softly*) Because, in the end, no matter what
    our troubles may be, those are the only things which see us through.
Monster (*dryly*) Together with a good many clichés, sir!

Talbot suddenly reappears on the staircase looking completely normal

Talbot (*delighted*) Zowee, powee, Holy Cow! Will you folks take a look at
    me now!!
Countess You're *normal*, Mr Talbot!
Talbot (*grinning*) You bet! (*Spinning round*) No tusks, no tufts, no tail—
    nothin'! Halleluia, brother!
Isabel Pity. I thought it was sexy!
Phantom (*shocked*) *Cherie*!
Isabel (*taking his hand*) Sorry, Maestro!
Talbot (*advancing to* C) I don't know about you guys, but this boy's in the
    mood for a party!
Frau Lurker (*askance*) What—*here*?

Talbot Aw, c'mon lady—we've all got somethin' to celebrate. An' this place ain't all that bad. In fact, when you think of the dumps most of us have hung out in—
Count (*ruefully*) Graveyards!
Ygor (*ruefully*) Belltowers!
Phantom (*ruefully*) Sewers!
Countess (*ruefully*) And Milton Keynes!!
Talbot —Man, it's paradise! So let's hit it!

There is general enthusiastic agreement and then a strange male voice cuts across the noise

Voice (*with a camp drawl*) Excuse me—is *anyone* invited?

Everyone looks up and around them, but Talbot jumps as if he has been "goosed"

Talbot What the—?!
Baron (*staring upwards*) Who—who said that?
Voice (*slyly*) *I* did!

Isabel squeals as if she, too has been "goosed"

Baroness But—where are you?
Voice Right behind you!

The Baron and the Baroness jump apart, staring in alarm at the gap between them

Baron (*realizing*) Man—you're *invisible*!
Baroness (*prodding the air and recoiling*) And you're *naked*!!
Voice (*suggestively*) Yes . . . I'm The Invisible Naked Man! And I just adore parties!!
Baron }
Baroness } (*together; as if they have been "goosed"*) Oh!!
Voice (*lecherously*) Heh, heh, heh!

There is a second's dumbfounded silence and then:

All (*wildly*) Let me out of here!!

They all race for the doors as The Voice chuckles again and—

the CURTAIN *falls*

FURNITURE AND PROPERTY LIST

exterior backing

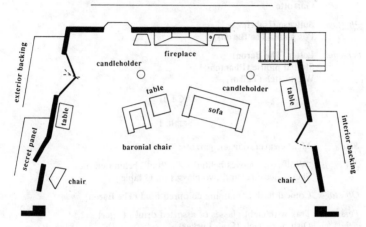

ACT I

SCENE 1

On stage: Large baronial chair
Old fashioned sofa with cushions
Four library chairs
Small table (centre)
Small table (right) *On it:* oil lamp
Small table (left) *On it:* a pile of books
Two large, freestanding, iron candleholders
Massive stone fireplace. *On mantelpiece:* two silver candelabra; preserving jars containing eyeballs, brains etc.; mounted human skull. *Over mantel:* Frankenstein coat of arms. *Beside mantel:* bell-rope
Worn carpet
Heavy floor length curtains with tapestry tie-backs
Over doors: animal heads
On walls: shields, maces, axes

Off stage: Glass beaker full of hot water **(Monster)**
Bloodstained meat cleaver **(Frau Lurker)**
Wet umbrella **(Baroness)**
Rucksack and crash-helmet **(Talbot)**
Tray with sherry decanter and six glasses **(Monster)**

Personal: Conical flask containing Minestrone Cup-A-Soup **(The Baron)**
Letter **(The Baron)**

SCENE 2

Strike: Conical flask and beaker

Personal: Two letters (Phantom)

SCENE 3

Set: Meat cleaver
             Dagger
             Garrotte

Off stage: Suitcase (Isabel)
             Pot plant (The Baron)

Personal: Letter (The Baron)
             Stuffed mouse (Phantom)
             Wristwatch (Talbot)

ACT II

SCENE 1

Strike: Meat cleaver, dagger, garrotte

Set: "Wolf paw" gloves behind sofa; "tail" behind cushion
             Sherry decanter and two glasses on C table

Off stage: Conical flask containing coloured fluid (The Baron)

Personal: Tray with eight glasses of assorted drinks (Ygor)
             Dish of pretzels (Frau Lurker)
             Lampshade and torch (Monster)

SCENE 2

Off stage: Cross (Ygor)
             Garlic cloves (Frau Lurker)
             Meat cleaver (Baroness)
             Revolver, firing blanks (The Baron)

SCENE 3

Strike: Tray
             Nine dirty glasses
             Pretzel dish
             Conical flask

Off stage: Suitcase (Baroness)

Personal: Turnip watch, fob and chain (The Baron)

SCENE 4

Off stage: Tray with eight glasses of lager (Monster)

Personal: Revolver, firing blanks (The Baron)

LIGHTING PLOT

No property fittings required

Interior. The Great Hall at Castle Frankenstein. The same scene throughout

ACT I, Scene 1. Early evening

To open: Fading sunlight and long shadows

Cue 1	**Baron:** "... create *LIFE*!!" *Vivid lightning flashes*	(Page 2)
Cue 2	**Baron:** "... but not impossible ..." *Slow fade to sunset*	(Page 9)
Cue 3	**Ygor:** "Sorry, Master!" *Sunset complete. Enhance candlelit areas*	(Page 13)
Cue 4	**Monster** shuffles miserably *Black-out*	(Page 14)

ACT I, Scene 2. Evening

To open: Evening lighting

Cue 5	**Count** enters *Blue light on area by doors* UR	(Page 16)
Cue 6	**Baron:** enters *Blue light fades out*	(Page 17)
Cue 7	**Baron:** "... she's to be made very welcome!" *Black-out*	(Page 20)

ACT I, Scene 3. Evening

To open: Evening lighting

Cue 8	**Count** strides towards staircase *Black-out*	(Page 28)

ACT II, Scene 1. Evening

To open: Evening lighting

Cue 9	**Baron:** "... the next calamity will be *yours*!!" *Slow fade to black-out*	(Page 33)

ACT II, Scene 2

To open: Evening lighting

Cue 10	**Baron** exits *Black-out*	(Page 35)

ACT III, SCENE 3.   One o'clock in the morning

To open: General lighting

Cue 11	**Talbot** and **The Phantom** exit	(Page 41)
	Black-out	

ACT II, SCENE 4.   A few minutes later

To open: General lighting

Cue 12	**Baron:** "I need more time!"	(Page 43)
	Lightning flashes	

Cue 13	**Baron:** "... made my night!"	(Page 43)
	Lightning flashes	

Cue 14	**Baron:** "... brink of *success*!"	(Page 44)
	Lightning flashes	

Cue 15	**Baron:** "... married a screwball!!"	(Page 44)
	Lightning flashes	

Cue 16	**Isabel:** "That's a new one ..."	(Page 44)
	Lightning flashes	

Cue 17	**All** race for the doors	(Page 48)
	Slow fade to Black-out	

EFFECTS PLOT

ACT I

Cue 1   Prior to CURTAIN rising   (Page 1)
         Menacing music

Cue 2   Following lightning flash   (Page 2)
         Thunder rolls

Cue 3   **Baroness**: "Oh, Victor—!"   (Page 4)
         Clock strikes seven

Cue 4   **Monster** exits   (Page 5)
         Motor bike pulls up, footsteps on gravel, doorbell

Cue 5   **Talbot**: "I turn into a *wolf*!"   (Page 7)
         Dramatic chord

Cue 6   **Baron** tugs bell-rope   (Page 9)
         Bell rings offstage

Cue 7   **Baron** exits   (Page 10)
         Carriage arrives, door opens and closes, footsteps on gravel and
            loud pounding on doors

Cue 8   **Monster** moves in a circle   (Page 10)
         Doorbell rings

Cue 9   **Ygor**: "And don't answer back!"   (Page 10)
         Doorbell rings

Cue 10   **Countess**: ". . . am a *vampire*!"   (Page 12)
         Dramatic chord

Cue 11   **Baron** tugs bell-rope   (Page 13)
         Bell rings offstage

Cue 12   Ten seconds after Lights come up   (Page 14)
         Gust of wind

Cue 13   **Barron**: "*What the*—?!"   (Page 15)
         Phantom's voice over as script plus organ music Fade

Cue 14   **Baron**: "Quiet, all of you!"   (Page 15)
         Loud knocking on outer doors

Cue 15   **Baron**: "Don't be idiotic!"   (Page 16)
         Loud knocking on outer doors

Cue 16   **Baron**: "I'm just going to put this somewhere safe!"   (Page 16)
         Loud knocking on outer doors

Cue 17	**Count:** "I am already *dead!*" *Dramatic chord*	(Page 17)
Cue 18	**Count:** "I beg your pardon?" *Amused chuckle from The Phantom offstage*	(Page 17)
Cue 19	**Baron** tugs bell-rope *Bell rings offstage*	(Page 19)
Cue 20	**Baron:** "... make her *very welcome* ..." *Phantom's voice over plus organ music*	(Page 20)
Cue 21	**Phantom:** "... 'and on a slug!" *Fade organ*	(Page 20)
Cue 22	**Baron:** "This is insane ..." *Loud knocking on outer doors*	(Page 20)
Cue 23	When the lights come up *Loud knocking on outer doors*	(Page 21)
Cue 24	As **Isabel** enters *1930s show music plays*	(Page 21)
Cue 25	**Isabel:** "He *is* MAD!!" *Insane laugh from The Phantom offstage*	(Page 22)
Cue 26	**Isabel:** "—if you insist ..." *Phantom's voice over*	(Page 22)
Cue 27	**Countess:** "Come here—big boy!" *Saxophone plays "the blues"*	(Page 26)
Cue 28	**Count** exits *Macabre music*	(Page 28)

ACT II

Cue 29	As Curtain rises *Music—Menacing, then up-tempo 30s dance rhythm*	(Page 29)
Cue 30	**Isabel:** "Go to it, Drac!" *Classical pas de deux plays*	(Page 29)
Cue 31	**All:** "Happiness and Normality!" *Phantom's voice over*	(Page 32)
Cue 32	**Phantom:** "... will now occur!!" *The clock strikes twelve*	(Page 32)
Cue 33	The **Count** exits *Sinister organ music begins*	(Page 33)
Cue 34	**Baron:** "... will be *yours!!*" *Phantom laughs maniacally and Organ music plays out*	(Page 33)
Cue 35	As Scene 2 begins *Up-tempo 30s music throughout action*	(Page 34)
Cue 36	When the Lights come up *Wolf howl followed by scream*	(Page 35)

Cue 37	**Phantom:** "... never live as one, together ..." *Wolf howl followed by scream and yell*	(Page 37)
Cue 38	**Ygor:** "Thanks!" *Wolf howl*	(Page 37)
Cue 39	**Baron:** "She'll know what to do—!" *Wolf howl followed by scream*	(Page 38)
Cue 40	**Baron** (angrily) "Damn!" *Wolf howl*	(Page 39)
Cue 41	As SCENE 4 opens *Bats flying and calling*	(Page 41)
Cue 42	**Countess:** "Indeed we shall." *Distant roll of thunder*	(Page 43)
Cue 43	**Count:** "Not good at all!" *Roll of thunder*	(Page 43)
Cue 44	**Baron:** "Phantom—you're dead!!" *Roll of thunder*	(Page 43)
Cue 45	**Count:** "And a very definite failure!" *Roll of thunder*	(Page 44)
Cue 46	**Baron:** "Stay away from me!" *Crash of thunder*	(Page 45)
Cue 47	**Baron:** "NO!!" *Terrific crash of thunder*	(Page 45)
Cue 48	**Baroness:** "Spare him ..." *Fading thunder*	(Page 46)
Cue 49	**Baroness** tugs bell-rope *Bell rings offstage*	(Page 46)
Cue 50	**Talbot:** "So let's hit it!" *Invisible man voice over (timed to dialogue)*	(Page 48)
Cue 51	**All** race for the doors *Closing music*	(Page 48)

A list of the music which formed the soundtrack of the original production may be obtained form Samuel French Ltd on request.

COSTUME SUGGESTIONS

Although the play is set in the present day, it will have more impact if it is costumed to resemble the fashions seen in the old horror films. Here are a few ideas:

The Baron. Edwardian daywear under laboratory coat. Evening tails, white tie etc. Turnip watch, fob and chain.

Ygor. Collarless shirt which is too long in the sleeves and which hangs out of his trousers. Scruffy trousers and shoes. Dusty tailcoat.

Monster. Drab jacket (too small), shirt, trousers (too short), and outsize shoes.

Frau Lurker. Victorian housekeeper's dress—black, with no fripperies. (Apron—preferably bloodstained).

Baroness. Victorian riding habit plus crop. Evening dress plus jewellery.

Talbot. Chinos, T-shirt and leather jacket. Tuxedo, dress shirt, black trousers and bow tie. (See *Special Effects* for further details.)

Countess. Georgian travelling outfit, hat and gloves. Evening dress and diamonds.

Phantom. White tie, tails, gloves, opera cloak and mask.

Count. Cavalier shirt, waistcoat, black frock coat, black neck band (over collar), cummerbund, floor length cloak with upturned collar.

Isabel. "Twenties" daywear plus hat and gloves. "Twenties" evening wear plus beads.

SPECIAL EFFECTS

Count Dracula. Although he *could* wear fangs throughout it would be more effective if these were affixed between Acts and revealed fully at the end of Act Two Scene 1. They should be long enough to be seen without them impeding his speech.
NB. The Countess does *not* require fangs.

Harry Talbot. His transformation into a werewolf is very simple. Between Acts he dons an undershirt and socks made out of grey "fun fur", which are hidden by his shoes and trouser cuffs. His fangs, like the Count's, should also be affixed during the interval, and he must try to conceal them until the transformation begins. When he sits on the sofa he attaches a rigid, bushy tail to the back of his trousers (hook over waistband). Once the transformation begins, having removed his shoes, he tears open his shirt (Velcro, not buttons) to reveal more fur. When he moves behind the sofa he quickly puts on a pair of "wolf paw" gloves which have been placed there during the interval just as the "tail" has been set behind a cushion on the sofa.

In Act Two Scene 3 he is yet more wolf-like, having stripped to the waist to fully reveal his fur-covered torso. He has also put on a close fitting wolf mask, complete with short muzzle and pointed ears. This should be lightweight and allow him to speak freely. When he becomes "normal" at the end of Act Two this is accomplished by him quickly stripping off his tail, gloves, socks, fangs and mask and donning a buttoned-up shirt.

The Phantom. His make-up need not be totally convincing. All that matters is the moustache and hair slicked over one eye. Of course, greater accuracy can be achieved if the make-up team care to try it. There are many photographs which will provide a model to work from.

The Monster. Model his make-up on Boris Karloff as *The Creature* from the first Frankenstein film. He should be pale, have a high forehead, square jaw, shadows round the eyes and, of course, the bolt through the neck. Hooded eyelids are effective.

The Vampires. Try to avoid using a white base make-up. This is never successful. Ivory is much more convincing, coupled with *some* shadows round the eyes. The eyes should be lined to make them seem "piercing". The Countess should have *carmine* lipstick, the Count *lake*. The ultimate effect should be one of "pale" humanity, rather than "bleached".

ADDITIONAL SUGGESTIONS

While there are many sound effects, a significant *visual* effect can be achieved through the use of *dry ice*, if this can be afforded. This should be used for the entrances of the Countess, The Phantom and the Count in Act One; to make the stage eerie at the beginning of Act Two Scenes 2, 3 and 4, and at the entrances of Talbot and The Phantom in Scene 4. The Baroness refers to fog in Act Two and this would make sense of her line.